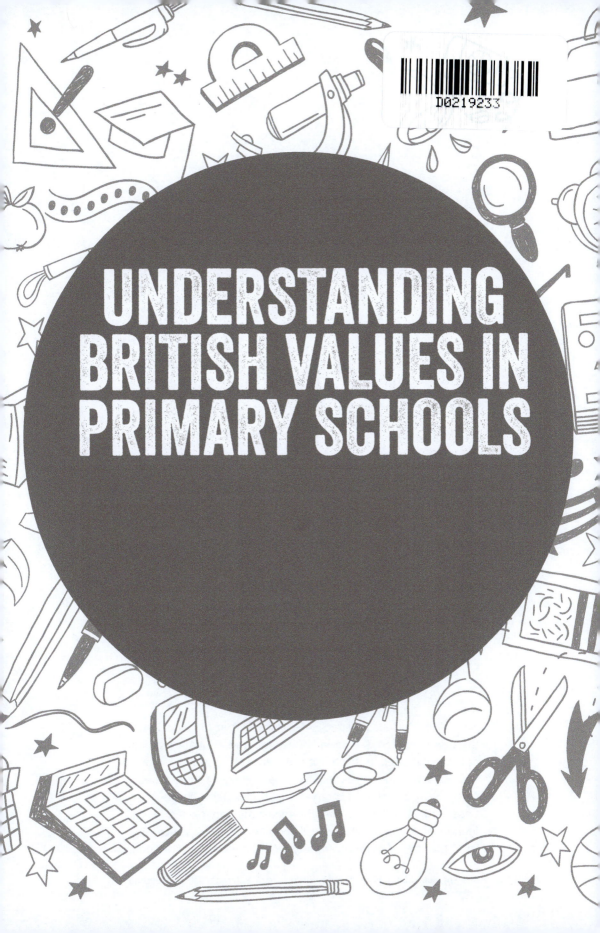

UNDERSTANDING BRITISH VALUES IN PRIMARY SCHOOLS

Sara Miller McCune founded SAGE Publishing in 1965 to support the dissemination of usable knowledge and educate a global community. SAGE publishes more than 1000 journals and over 800 new books each year, spanning a wide range of subject areas. Our growing selection of library products includes archives, data, case studies and video. SAGE remains majority owned by our founder and after her lifetime will become owned by a charitable trust that secures the company's continued independence.

Los Angeles | London | New Delhi | Singapore | Washington DC | Melbourne

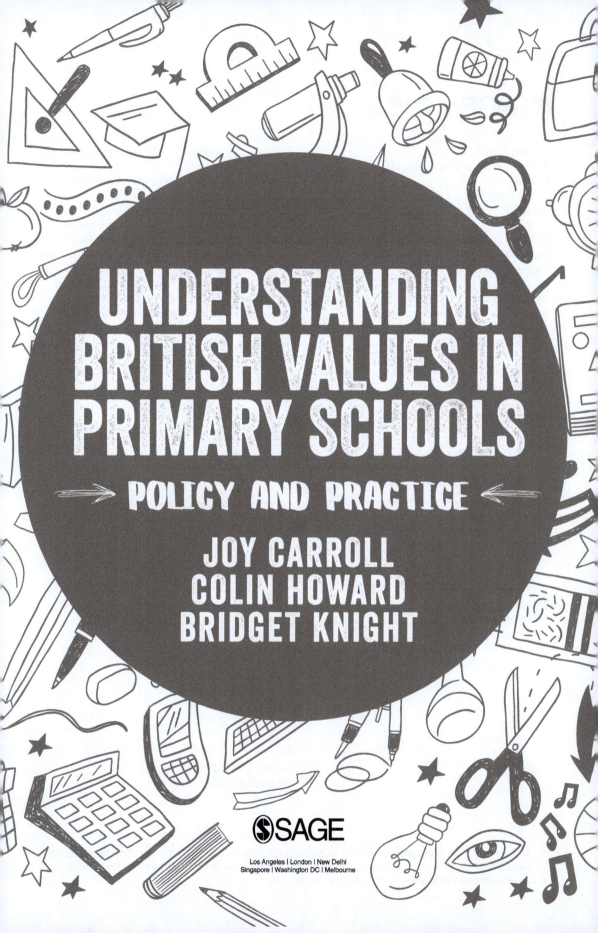

UNDERSTANDING BRITISH VALUES IN PRIMARY SCHOOLS

→ POLICY AND PRACTICE ←

JOY CARROLL
COLIN HOWARD
BRIDGET KNIGHT

$SAGE

Los Angeles | London | New Delhi
Singapore | Washington DC | Melbourne

Learning Matters
An imprint of SAGE Publications Ltd
1 Oliver's Yard
55 City Road
London EC1Y 1SP

SAGE Publications Inc.
2455 Teller Road
Thousand Oaks, California 91320

SAGE Publications India Pvt Ltd
B 1/I 1 Mohan Cooperative Industrial Area
Mathura Road
New Delhi 110 044

SAGE Publications Asia-Pacific Pte Ltd
3 Church Street
#10-04 Samsung Hub
Singapore 049483

Editor: Amy Thornton
Development editor: Jennifer Clark
Production controller: Chris Marke
Project management: Deer Park Productions
Marketing Manager: Dilhara Attygalle
Cover design: Wendy Scott
Typeset by: C&M Digitals (P) Ltd, Chennai, India
Printed in the UK

First edition published in 2018 by Learning Matters Ltd

Library of Congress Control Number: 2018933057

British Library Cataloguing in Publication Data

A catalogue record for this book is available from the British Library.

ISBN 978-1-5264-0840-2
ISBN 978-1-5264-0841-9 (pbk)

At SAGE we take sustainability seriously. Most of our products are printed in the UK using responsibly sourced papers and boards. When we print overseas we ensure sustainable papers are used as measured by the PREPS grading system. We undertake an annual audit to monitor our sustainability.

CONTENTS

ABOUT THE AUTHORS

Joy Carroll is a Senior Lecturer in Primary Initial Teacher Education (ITE) at the University of Worcester. She teaches on the undergraduate and post-graduate courses and is Partnership Placement Manager. Before moving into ITE she worked as a teacher and assistant headteacher in primary schools in London, Hereford, Worcester and Stafford and was the manager of a private nursery school. Following this, Joy worked as an advisor within the area of school workforce in a local authority, working closely with schools on deployment of support staff. She is currently working on doctoral research into how schools and universities work in partnership to support ITE.

Dr Colin Howard is a Senior Primary Lecturer in ITE at the University of Worcester. He has been involved in primary education in Herefordshire for over 24 years, of which 16 years have been as a successful head teacher in both small village and large primary school settings. He has been involved in inspecting schools for the Diocese of Hereford as a S48 SIAMS Inspector and has a strong research interest in teachers' professional identity.

Bridget Knight is in her third headship, now leading a renowned values-based primary school. For a number of years, her work was in local authority school improvement and, subsequently, in curriculum development at the Qualifications and Curriculum Development Agency (QCDA). Her guiding principle – helping children to 'grow roots and wings' – has inspired her throughout her career to examine the myriad ways in which educators can enable children and young people to flourish emotionally and spiritually. Her current role enables her to explore this philosophy first hand.

1

AN INTRODUCTION TO BRITISH VALUES IN PRIMARY SCHOOLS

This chapter explores:

- the definition of values in education, including British Values;
- the importance of values in education;
- the relationship between British Values and the National Curriculum 2014;
- strategies that promote the effective delivery of values-based education.

Teachers' Standards

This chapter is linked to the following Teachers' Standards and includes examples of how they can be integrated into the classroom:

TS1: Set high expectations which inspire, motivate and challenge pupils:

- a safe and stimulating environment for pupils, rooted in mutual respect;
- demonstrate consistently the positive attitudes, values and behaviour which are expected of pupils.

Part Two: Personal and professional conduct

Teachers uphold public trust in the profession and maintain high standards of ethics and behaviour, within and outside school, by:

- treating pupils with dignity, building relationships rooted in mutual respect, and at all times observing proper boundaries appropriate to a teacher's professional position;

- not undermining fundamental British Values, including democracy, the rule of law, individual liberty and mutual respect, and tolerance of those with different faiths and beliefs;

- ensuring that personal beliefs are not expressed in ways which exploit pupils' vulnerability or might lead them to break the law.

The introduction of the term 'fundamental British Values' within the Teachers' Standards has led to a growth and development of the subject (Lander, 2016). Interest has increased considerably, reaching all who are involved in education from initial teacher education through to qualified teachers, children, parents and governors.

The development and context of values in education

It is important that any examination of the requirement of schools to teach British Values is placed in the context of the historic debate surrounding values in education. The introduction of the promotion of British Values through education emerged in 2012 under the UK Coalition government. At this time it was conceived as part of a wider government agenda to seek to prevent vulnerable individuals being radicalised and therefore being drawn into terrorism (VICTVS, 2013; Department for Education and Lord Nash, 2014) as part of the government's ongoing Prevent Strategy agenda (HM Government, 2011). As part of this approach, schools are therefore now required to teach about and explore the British Values of democracy, the rule of law, individual liberty, and mutual respect and tolerance of those with different faiths and beliefs (Department for Education, 2014a).

The promotion of British Values through education and training must start with an agreement and shared understanding of what is meant by Britishness.

KEY QUESTIONS

- What is Britishness?
- What are British Values?

Questions have been raised about whether or not the values listed above are indeed distinctive to Britain (Maylor, 2016). Yet, to ensure the future of a society that is multi-ethnic it was deemed important to define what unites the people of Britain. A definition emerged that stated, 'To be British mean[s] that we respect the laws, the parliamentary and democratic political structures, traditional values of mutual tolerance, respect for equal rights' (Maylor, 2016).

The government aims to ensure that British Values are not undermined through a teacher's influence in the classroom (Maylor, 2016). As a teacher, you are a role model for children and their families, and as such you are a significant factor in promoting values and upholding trust. For many schools such an approach has meant a revisiting and remodelling of their current policy and practice around the humanistic or Christian values that often underpin schools.

The history of values in British education

Copley (2000, p.10) identifies that, in 1993, 'Spiritual and Moral Development – a discussion paper by the National Curriculum Council' (first issued by NCC in 1993, reissued by SCAA in 1995, p.5) identified component aspects of spiritual development: beliefs, experience of transience, inspiration from the natural world, mystery or human achievement, the search for meaning and purpose. It was also explicit about the moral values schools should promote, and those it should reject: bullying, cheating, deceit, cruelty, irresponsibility and dishonesty. Pupils should leave school able to articulate their own attitudes and values. Schools were therefore encouraged to agree and promote core values acceptable to all the community, but there was little guidance or resources to enable them to do this in a coherent and effective fashion.

The United Nations Convention on the Rights of the Child (1989), ratified by HM Government in 1991, gives significant endorsement to the notion of values (Office of the United Nations High Commissioner for Human Rights, 1989). Further, the establishment of the Values Education Council in the UK in 1995 aimed to bring together organisations with a shared interest in 'values education', its purpose being 'the promotion and development of values in the context of education as a lifelong process, to help individuals develop as responsible and caring persons and live as participating members of a pluralistic society' (Taylor, 1995, p.24, in Halstead and Taylor (eds), 1996, p.8).

This theme was espoused in the 1996 National Symposium, initiated by the School Curriculum and Assessment Authority (SCAA), which began a process of national consultation on the spiritual and moral dimensions of the curriculum. It set out to discover whether there were any values on which there was agreement across society and then to decide how society in general and SCAA in particular might best support spiritual, moral, social and cultural (SMSC) development. According to Deakin-Crick (2002, p.132), this was a landmark and raised the level of debate through a wide consultation process.

Educating for values or values education and its place in the primary school

The resurgence of interest in values education in the United Kingdom began way before British Values was conceptualised. It owes much to the statutory requirement that the SMSC development of pupils should be subject to official inspection.

British Values and their place within the OFSTED inspection agenda

The importance of values in education is endorsed by the School inspection handbook (OFSTED, 2017), which acts as a catalyst for schools to reappraise their values education. Inspectors must evaluate 'the effectiveness and impact of the provision for pupils' spiritual, moral, social and cultural development' (p.38).

The OFSTED Framework 'grades' provision and outcomes in the area through examining the effectiveness of the school's provision for SMSC education.

The School inspection handbook: handbook for inspecting schools in England under section 5 of the Education Act 2005 (OFSTED, 2017) requires inspectors to make key judgements of schools on the following areas:

- overall effectiveness;
- leadership and management;
- quality of teaching, learning and assessment;
- personal behaviour, development and welfare;
- outcomes for pupils.

The inspection handbook uses a four point scale:

Grade 1: outstanding

Grade 2: good

Grade 3: requires improvement

Grade 4: inadequate.

SMSC is threaded through all these key areas of judgement by OFSTED, sitting perhaps most explicitly in the section for personal behaviour, development and welfare.

The OFSTED handbook (2017, p.35) defines SMSC in the following terms with specific references to British Values:

The spiritual development of pupils is shown by their:

- ability to be reflective about their own beliefs, religious or otherwise, that inform their perspective on life and their interest in and respect for different people's faiths, feelings or values;

- sense of enjoyment and fascination in learning about themselves, others and the world around them;

- use of imagination and creativity in their learning;

- willingness to reflect on their experiences.

The moral development of pupils is shown by their:

- ability to recognise the difference between right and wrong and to readily apply this understanding in their own lives, recognise legal boundaries and, in so doing, respect the civil and criminal law of England;

- understanding of the consequences of their behaviour and actions;

- interest in investigating and offering reasoned views about moral and ethical issues and ability to understand and appreciate the viewpoints of others on these issues.

The social development of pupils is shown by their:

- use of a range of social skills in different contexts – for example, working and socialising with other pupils, including those from different religious, ethnic and socio-economic backgrounds;

- willingness to participate in a variety of communities and social settings, including by volunteering, cooperating well with others and being able to resolve conflicts effectively;

- acceptance and engagement with the fundamental British Values of democracy, the rule of law, individual liberty and mutual respect and tolerance of those with different faiths and beliefs; they develop and demonstrate skills and attitudes that will allow them to participate fully in and contribute positively to life in modern Britain.

The cultural development of pupils is shown by their:

- understanding and appreciation of the wide range of cultural influences that have shaped their own heritage and those of others;

- understanding and appreciation of the range of different cultures within school and further afield as an essential element of their preparation for life in modern Britain;

- knowledge of Britain's democratic parliamentary system and its central role in shaping our history and values, and in continuing to develop Britain;

- willingness to participate in and respond positively to artistic, musical, sporting and cultural opportunities;

- interest in exploring, improving understanding of and showing respect for different faiths and cultural diversity and the extent to which they understand, accept, respect and celebrate diversity, as shown by their tolerance and attitudes towards different religious, ethnic and socio-economic groups in the local, national and global communities.

In order for a school to be graded as outstanding it is essential that the school's thoughtful and wide-ranging promotion of pupils' SMSC development and their physical wellbeing enables pupils to thrive.

Curriculum links with British Values

Holden and Clough (1998, p.16) state that: 'A curriculum which develops the skills of critical reflection and assists values-based participation can begin to meet the identified needs of both children and society.' This has clear implications for the climate of schools and the particular ethos they generate so that schools do both reflect and influence their local communities and their particular needs.

The curriculum links with values are both implicit and explicit. As teachers we have a responsibility to show an awareness of how integrated British Values are and can be with the statutory curriculum – and to draw out the possibilities it implies. It is important to remind ourselves of how embedded values in education are, and what endless opportunities are afforded by the National Curriculum for England itself.

The National Curriculum 2014 (p.5) states the following:

> *Every state-funded school must offer a curriculum which is balanced and broadly based and which:*
>
> - *promotes the spiritual, moral, cultural, mental and physical development of pupils at the school and of society, and*
>
> - *prepares pupils at the school for the opportunities, responsibilities and experiences of later life.*

Table 1.1 exemplifies the links to teaching and learning about British Values that are embedded within the National Curriculum subjects.

Table 1.1 British Values: links to teaching and learning

Curriculum subject	Links to teaching and learning about British Values
English: spoken language	Discuss the meaning and impact of values through being increasingly able to: convey ideas clearly, justify ideas with reasons, check knowledge, negotiate, evaluate and build on the ideas of others; speculate, hypothesise and explore ideas.
English: reading and writing	Explore the meaning and impact of values through being increasingly able to: read and write widely in genres including narratives, explanations, descriptions, comparisons, summaries and evaluations.
English: vocabulary development	Discuss the meaning and impact of values through being increasingly able to: use expanding vocabulary choices to convey and comprehend ideas.
Mathematics	Explore the impact of values through application of geometric and algebraic understanding; understanding of probability to notions of risk and uncertainty; understand the cycle of collecting, presenting and analysing data.
Science	Develop understanding of the meaning and impact of values through scientific enquiry: observing over time; pattern seeking; identifying, classifying and grouping; comparative and fair testing (controlled investigations); and researching using secondary sources. Pupils should seek answers to questions through collecting, analysing and presenting data. Articulate these concepts clearly and precisely.
Art and design	See how values can be represented in cultures and through time by developing the ability to think critically; know how art and design both reflect and shape our history, and contribute to the culture, creativity and wealth of our nation. Be able to analyse creative works using the language of art, craft and design.
Citizenship (secondary schools only)	A high-quality citizenship education helps to provide pupils with knowledge, skills and understanding to prepare them to play a full and active part in society. In particular, citizenship education should foster pupils' keen awareness and understanding of democracy, government and how laws are made and upheld. Teaching should equip pupils with the skills and knowledge to explore political and social issues critically, to weigh evidence, debate and make reasoned arguments.
Computing	Examine the role of values through being increasingly digitally literate – able to use, and express themselves and develop their ideas through, information and communication technology.
Design and technology	The skills developed in this subject promote pupils' ability to critique, evaluate and test their ideas and the work of others – and therefore to bring this critical thinking ability to matters involving values.

(Continued)

Table 1.1 (Continued)

Curriculum subject	Links to teaching and learning about British Values
Geography	Inspire engagement in consideration of our own and others' values: a high-quality geography education should inspire in pupils a curiosity and fascination about the world and its people that will remain with them for the rest of their lives. In thinking about values pupils need to be able to apply the skills of analysis, communication and interpretation to a range of data and information.
History	Develop in pupils the cognitive ability to analyse and formulate ideas in the consideration of their own and others' values. Teaching should equip pupils to ask perceptive questions, think critically, weigh evidence, sift arguments, and develop perspective and judgement. History helps pupils to understand the complexity of people's lives, the process of change, the diversity of societies and relationships between different groups, as well as their own identity and the challenges of their time. All these skills and processes are essential to the relationship pupils will need to develop with their own, other people and society's values.
Languages	Learning a foreign language is a liberation from insularity and provides an opening to other cultures. A high-quality languages education should foster pupils' curiosity and deepen their understanding of the world. The skills and processes involved in learning another language are therefore critical to whole-hearted and deep engagement with discussion about the meaning and value of values.
Music	The National Curriculum describes this as the 'universal language'. The music curriculum can be actively and purposefully used to help pupils to see and appreciate commonality between races, cultures, faiths and genders.
Physical education	Opportunities to compete in sport and other activities build character and help to embed values such as fairness and respect.

The idea of teaching about values is by no means new or original. Schools have been attending to these for many years, either explicitly or implicitly. The notion of British Values as a mainstay, however, is relatively recent. Other than the defined British Values, educational legislation leaves largely undefined the acceptable personal qualities and values that pupils should espouse. However, many teachers understand that for children to be and become vibrant and successful they must acquire a set of myriad skills that will enable them to face and overcome the challenges they will undoubtedly meet.

Increasingly, schools in this country and across the world are recognising that a whole school approach to the teaching of values is the most effective way forward. Values education, as a particular approach to ensuring the central position of spiritual, moral and social education in primary schools, has been developed by some schools in Oxfordshire (Hawkes, 2002, and Farrer, 2000) and is being taken up nationally, and internationally, with continued passion. The guidance developed in Hawkes (2002) was inspired by a UNICEF project entitled: *Living Values: A Guidebook* (Naraine, 1995). The Living Values programme was developed at a meeting of educators from around the world who discussed how values could be integrated in education to prepare students for life-long learning and to counter developing trends towards violence, social problems and a lack of respect for one another and the world.

For these schools, a whole school approach to a values-based education is a holistic matter. As educators they believe they have been given the privilege and opportunity to place before pupils rich possibilities, and to furnish them with a lifetime's gift of intellectual, moral, emotional and spiritual intelligences. For such schools, the teaching of British Values is therefore not a 'bolt-on' exercise, but part of a wider philosophy that infuses pedagogy and principles.

Theirs is a deeply practical approach to a more socially inclusive, motivating and rewarding school experience, enabling learners to flourish and become engaged and motivated citizens of their country and the world.

Adopting a whole school approach

Many schools opt to embrace an approach defined by Dr Neil Hawkes (2002, 2015) called 'values-based education'. It works by establishing and maintaining a school ethos and culture that emphasises:

- the development of shared values and associated language;
- the facilitation of philosophical dialogue and debate;
- the conscious and explicit modelling of positive behaviour and cognitive traits;
- the emphasis on personal endeavour and spiritual reflection;
- attention to a broad and balanced values-based curriculum;
- the centrality of positive relationships and a harmonious ethos.

Often, these schools will begin their mission by agreeing a set of values. These work like a set of principles. An early and very powerful activity is to ask each pupil/ staff member/governor/parent to come up with their top five values – the ones that appear on everyone's list can become your school's chosen values.

KEY QUESTIONS

- What values would be listed as your 'top five'?
- Are these different from those of your colleagues?

Some schools like to use a Diamond Nine activity. This is when a series of values are chosen and then ranked in order of their importance. This creates discussion and agreement on the school's values. The cards below offer an example of values that can be used for this activity. Remember you must be prepared to justify your reasoning. People quickly realise that each has merit and that all interrelate: the word itself is just the starting point for the values exploration. It's a great way to get going! Some cards are deliberately left blank so that people can suggest their own ideas. Values – such as justice, for example – can be deliberately included to ensure a commonality with the defined British Values.

Peace	Respect	Love
Tolerance	Care	Hope
Happiness	?	Trust
Humility	Unity	?
Understanding	Justice	Simplicity

Children are exposed to these values through dialogue, discussion and modelling, thereby acquiring an ethical vocabulary through which they can observe, analyse and interpret the world. Through this ethical vocabulary, they develop ethical thinking, which leads to ethical relationships. Relationships across the school are key.

The facilitation of philosophical dialogue and debate

Discussion and dialogue is seen as a critical component of this approach. The teaching approach is facilitative: this is not about 'right' answers and 'wrong' answers – this is about encouraging children to become critical thinkers, actively analysing and creating hypotheses and even solutions and, most importantly of all, identifying themselves as people who have views about their world. Look how one primary school plans for a deep journey through one value.

CARE – example 'thought shower' for planning over a term:

- **Caring for ourselves** – exercise, diet, personal hygiene, drugs, self-respect, self-esteem, self-confidence, personal goals, high standards, being true to ourselves.
- **How do we show we care?** – giving time, listening, actions, cards and presents, prayers, words, looking after pets, charities, pressure groups.
- **Caring role models** – family, friends, Jesus, Mother Theresa, Nelson Mandela, Florence Nightingale, community members, caring professions.
- **What do you care about?** – priorities, materialism, taking action, taking control.
- **Caring for the world** – environment, people in other countries, living in harmony.
- **Caring structures** – UN Charter: The Rights of the Child, laws and government, Samaritans, Childline.

KEY QUESTIONS

- How does this journey through the value of care enable children to acquire a greater sophistication of thinking as well as a depth of understanding?
- How could this approach be used to focus children's thinking on distinctly British Values?
- How can it become part of an organised curriculum?

The conscious and explicit modelling of positive behaviour and cognitive traits

In following the outlined approach, staff adopt a heightened awareness that we all, and children especially, will – consciously and unconsciously – adopt and mimic the behaviour traits and attitudes of those around us. Therefore, they are mindful of their own ethical behaviour, resisting shouting, using affirmative language and being kind, caring and compassionate in their daily work. Hawkes (2002, 2015) says this has the greatest impact of all the strategies combined in this work.

The emphasis on personal endeavour and spiritual reflection

Some schools have 'values for learning', which encourage pupils to adopt certain mental outlooks in order to get the most from schooling. These may chime with certain other values including determination, resilience and care. A principal component of the values-based approach is the development of a spiritual consciousness through the use of processes such as stilling or reflection. Taking part in daily or regular reflection activities involving calming of the body and mind, perhaps through visualisation times, develops inner and outer harmony and a maturity of thought and emotion.

CASE STUDY: REFLECTION

In one primary school, reflection is the part of the assembly that the children look forward to most. It has its own rituals and ceremony that are quickly understood by the whole school.

A relaxed, calm atmosphere is created using dimmed lighting and calming music.

The leader models the required behaviour, being seated and calm, and gently smiling at the pupils.

Pupils are taught how to sit in a still, relaxed, alert and comfortable manner. This is consistently modelled by the teacher, who demonstrates how to sit in a relaxed but alert manner.

They are then reminded and shown how to place their hands in their laps.

The children are asked to close their eyes or focus on a candle light. They are invited to focus on their breaths.

The children are then invited to engage in a short period of reflection (a minute can be enough) about someone they love, doing something they like and so on, related to the value under discussion.

Pupils here have gradually developed the ability to be especially still and to then go within themselves, and experience their inner life. During the reflection time at this school there is a beautiful tranquility and children speak readily and cogently about how these times enable them to 'feel calm', 'be at peace' and 'think my own thoughts'.

The attention to the broad and balanced values-based curriculum

Many schools will deliberately seek out opportunities to develop their pupils' understanding of values through their lessons and curriculum provision. Some schools use a planning pro forma that alerts you to make explicit opportunities to weave in a values-based focus. Some schools will have written in to their principles for planning a requirement that planning at all levels makes provision for the development of understanding and application of school and British Values (including Prevent) alongside and or through SMSC education (see Table 1.2). Many of these schools too will create a carefully planned curriculum for personal

Table 1.2 Planning for British Values

Anywhere Primary School Medium Term Subject Plan

Subject:	Year group(s):
Topic/theme:	Term and year:
Context/prior learning:	Provision notes for PPG/vulnerable groups:
Provision notes for SEN:	Provision notes for more able:

Outside speakers/visits/experiences:

Key concept/ question	Learning outcomes (differentiated)	Learning activity and content (incl. ICT)	Homework/ extended learning opportunities	Approximate time	Resources	Opportunities to develop values/ SMSC/extended writing/maths	Assessment, based on success criteria

and social education which, although no longer a statutory part of the National Curriculum 2014, enables schools to address a variety of factors in which values play an important part.

The centrality of positive relationships and a harmonious ethos

The combined effect of this kind of focus is borne out across a whole school. Numerous schools cite its positive effect in bringing about whole school positive change.

CASE STUDY: VALUES EDUCATION AND BEHAVIOUR

The current headteacher cited problems with behaviour as a major reason for introducing values-based education into the school. The school now follows the method of values education outlined in Hawkes (2002) in which the basic elements are agreeing and discussing a set of values via an examination of words, such as 'peace', 'honesty' and 'cooperation', in assemblies and lessons. A month is spent on each value. The staff take the lead in role-modelling the desired behaviour of their pupils, leading them on a journey of self-discovery and understanding through discussion and the use of quiet reflection or visualisation times. The school's work on values is shared with parents. It is considered to be a whole school approach and a philosophical way of being which will enhance the individual's personal and educational experience. Renewed thought and care is given to the outdoor and indoor environment. In the playground are newly made flower gardens (created by a parent, staff and children working party) with gravel paths and a 'quiet time' bench in one corner. This sense of affirmation in the shared areas of the school is echoed in the classrooms. The collective symbolism of the displays, choice of language and coherent emphasis on affirmation all speak of this. In every class, in fact, is a values display. In the Year 6 classroom (the headteacher's class) is a poster that offers '100 ways to praise a child'. There is a sofa in one corner - the 'chill out zone' - together with beautiful and carefully created displays of natural objects. On walls are inspiring quotations from famous people, such as the Nelson Mandela quote on the Year 6 classroom door, 'Stand up for what is right, even if you stand alone.' The children have made a 'dream teacher' and a 'dream pupil' poster that list the qualities they admire. Overall, this classroom communicates great care and respect for the individuals in the class. The behaviours of the children in this school are influenced by the calm manner in which the teachers choose to manage their classes and lead by example. Children now expect - and are expected - to behave well. There is an emphasis on speaking, not shouting, on listening to children and on enjoying them as individuals. The children understand this and respond in kind. Particularly striking is the relationship between the teacher and their class. The relationship is one of equality, and is fully appreciated by the boys and girls alike; at the end of term, one child dedicated a song to the headteacher, saying that the headteacher was 'gold in her life'.

Values into action!

How do I transfer this to the classroom? Below is a list of ways in which you can put this into action in your school or classroom:

- set up a programme for whole staff training;

- decide your core values together with children, staff, parents and governors. Think about how explicitly British Values can be accommodated here;

- audit where these values are already in evidence in your school;

- create posters and displays for the school: make the implicit explicit;

- use values as the basis for planning for assemblies;

- create your school's values statement;

- tell parents about values through a newsletter or create a values leaflet;

- introduce reflection times;

- incorporate values into curriculum planning and lessons. It can be helpful to have a planning pro forma that requires the link to values to be made – it focuses thinking;

- write your values into your school aims and policies;

- go on a 'values learning walk' to audit and develop practice;

- keep thinking and talking about them.

KEY QUESTIONS

- What do you want to be your guiding principles that govern your approach to the teaching and delivery of values, including British Values?
- What approaches can you employ to ensure that this learning is meaningful and effective?
- How will you get all your staff on board with your plans?

A SUMMARY OF KEY POINTS FROM THIS CHAPTER

- The promotion of British Values through education and training must start with an agreement and shared understanding of what is meant by Britishness.
- Teachers are role models for children and their families, and as such are a significant factor in promoting values and upholding trust.

(Continued)

- There is an explicit requirement upon schools to address values including British Values as part of the curriculum.
- Schools must successfully and effectively address these values in order to meet the requirements of OFSTED.
- A whole school values-based ethos and approach is irreplaceable in terms of what it gives to school communities.
- Knowledge, understanding and learning about specifically British Values and their implications is critical.

References

Citizenship Foundation (2015) What are British Values? Available at: http://www.doingsmsc.org.uk/british-values/ (accessed 9 November 2016).

Clough, N. and Holden, C. (eds) (1998) *Children as Citizens: Education for Participation.* London: Jessica Kingsley.

Copley, T. (2000) *Spiritual Development in the State School.* Exeter: University of Exeter Press.

Deakin-Crick, R. (2002) *Transforming Visions: Managing Values in Schools, A Case Study.* London: Middlesex University Press.

Department for Education (2012) Teachers' Standards. DFE-00066-2011. London: Department for Education.

Department for Education (2014a) Promoting fundamental British Values as part of SMSC in schools: departmental advice for maintained schools. Available at: https://www.gov.uk/government/uploads/system/uploads/attachment_data/file/380595/SMSC_Guidance_Maintained_Schools.pdf (accessed 6 November 2016).

Department for Education (2014b) National Curriculum for England Framework Document, DfE. Department for Education and Lord Nash (2014) Guidance on promoting British Values in schools published. Available at: https://www.gov.uk/government/news/guidance-on-promoting-british-values-in-schools-published (accessed 7 November 2016).

Foundation Years (2015) Fundamental British Values in the Early Years. Available at: http://www.foundationyears.org.uk/files/2015/03/Fundamental_British_Values.pdf (accessed 7 November 2016).

Halstead, J.M. and Taylor, M.J. (1996) *Values in Education and Education in Values.* Abingdon: RoutledgeFalmer.

HM Government (2011) *Prevent* Strategy. Available at: https://www.gov.uk/govern ment/uploads/system/uploads/attachment_data/file/97976/prevent-strategy-review. pdf (accessed 1 January 2017).

Kahn, F. (2016) 'Combining the Equality Act with a whole-school ethos to deliver British Values'. *Race Equality Teaching*, 34 (1): 26–31.

Lander, V. (2016) 'Introduction to fundamental British Values'. *Journal of Education for Teaching*, 42 (3): 274–9.

Maylor, U. (2016) '"I'd worry about how to teach it": British Values in English class-rooms'. *Journal of Education for Teaching*, 42 (3): 314–28.

Office of the United Nations High Commissioner for Human Rights (1989) Convention on the Rights of the Child. Available at: http://www.ohchr.org/ Documents/ProfessionalInterest/crc.pdf (accessed 18 December 2017).

OFSTED (2017) School inspection handbook: handbook for inspecting schools in England under section 5 of the Education Act 2005, OFSTED.

QCA (1999) National Curriculum for Schools. London: QCA.

'Spiritual and Moral Development – a discussion paper by the National Curriculum Council' (first issued by NCC in 1993, reissued by SCAA in 1995, p.5).

Sutrop, M. (2015) 'Can values be taught? The myth of value-free education'. *Trames*, 19 (2): 189–202.

VICTVS (2013) Helping you to promote fundamental British Values in school. Available at: https://www.victvs.co.uk/british-values/ (accessed 7 November 2016).

Recommended reading

Department for Education (2014b) National Curriculum for England. London: DfE.

Duckworth, J. (2009) *The Little Book of Values: Educating Children to Become Thinking, Responsible and Caring Citizens*. Carmarthen: Crown House.

Farrer, F. (2000) *A Quiet Revolution*. London: Rider.

Hawkes, N. (2002) *How to Inspire and Develop Positive Values in Your Classroom*. Cambridge: LDA.

Hawkes, N. (2015) *From My Heart: Transforming Lives Through Values*. Carmarthen: Crown House.

Naraine, G. (1995) *Living Values: A Guidebook*. San Francisco: Brahma Kumaris.

OFSTED (2016) *Handbook for Schools in England*. London: OFSTED.

2
DEMOCRACY

This chapter explores:

- the definition of democracy in Britain as part of the British Values requirements;
- the role that democracy plays in the life of the school and the curriculum;
- the importance of teaching about democracy in the primary school;
- the relationship between safeguarding and the delivery of democracy in Britain as part of the British Values;
- strategies that promote the effective delivery of the teaching of democracy.

Teachers' Standards

This chapter supports the development of the following Teachers' Standards:

TS1: Set high expectations which inspire, motivate and challenge pupils:

- a safe and stimulating environment for pupils, rooted in mutual respect.

TS7: Manage behaviour effectively to ensure a good and safe learning environment:

- have clear rules and routines for behaviour in the classroom, and take responsibility for promoting good and courteous behaviour both in the classroom and around the school, in accordance with the school's behaviour policy.

Part Two: Personal and professional conduct

Teachers uphold public trust in the profession and maintain high standards of ethics and behaviour, within and outside school, by:

- treating pupils with dignity, building relationships rooted in mutual respect, and at all times observing proper boundaries appropriate to a teacher's professional position;

- show tolerance and respect for the rights of others;

- not undermining fundamental British Values, including democracy, the rule of law, individual liberty and mutual respect, and tolerance of those with different faiths and beliefs;

- ensuring that personal beliefs are not expressed in ways which exploit pupils' vulnerability or might lead them to break the law.

Introduction

This chapter will focus on defining democracy and examining the role it now plays in aspects of our daily lives in schools. Whilst recognising how the historical context has shaped the notion of democracy, the main focus of this chapter is concerned with how the idea of democracy is understood by children and the strategies that allow for its integration and enactment within the school context.

'Every child has the right to say what they think in all matters affecting them, and have their views taken seriously' (UN Convention on the Rights of the Child, Article 12).

The relationship between the National Curriculum and British Values: democracy

Although personal, social and health education (PSHE) is non-compulsory in primary schools, many teachers find this is a vital component of a broad and balanced curriculum. Table 2.1 outlines the links between the concept of democracy with elements that schools would address through their PSHE (PSHE Association, 2016). As you will see, there are many similarities between teaching for democracy and teaching for the rule of law.

Table 2.1 Links to the National Curriculum: democracy

PSHE Key Stage 1	• Know that they belong to various groups and communities such as family and school. • Know about Children's Rights and Human Rights. • Share opinions on things that matter to them and explain their views through discussions. • Listen to other people and play and work cooperatively (including strategies to resolve simple arguments through negotiation). • Recognise what they like and dislike, how to make real, informed choices that improve their physical and emotional health. • Recognise that choices can have good and not so good consequences. • Recognise what is fair and unfair, kind and unkind, what is right and wrong. • Recognise when people are being unkind either to them or others.
PSHE Key Stage 2	• Know how to make informed choices (including recognising that choices can have positive, neutral and negative consequences) and to begin to understand the concept of a 'balanced lifestyle'. • Research, discuss and debate topical issues, problems and events concerning health and wellbeing and offer their recommendations to appropriate people. • Reflect on and celebrate their achievements, identify their strengths, areas for improvement, set high aspirations and goals. • Recognise that they may experience conflicting emotions and when they might need to listen to their emotions or overcome them. • Understand that everyone has human rights, all peoples and all societies, and that children have their own special rights set out in the United Nations Declaration of the Rights of the Child. • Recognise that they share a responsibility for keeping themselves and others safe, when to say, 'yes', 'no', 'I'll ask' and 'I'll tell'. • Know that these universal rights are there to protect everyone and have primacy both over national law and family and community practices. • Realise the consequences of anti-social and aggressive behaviours such as bullying and discrimination of individuals and communities. • Know that there are different kinds of responsibilities, rights and duties at home, at school, in the community and towards the environment. • Resolve differences by looking at alternatives, seeing and respecting others' points of view, making decisions and explaining choices. • Appreciate role of voluntary, community and pressure groups, especially in relation to health and wellbeing. • Know that resources can be allocated in different ways and that these economic choices affect individuals, communities and sustainability. • Explore and critique how the media present information. • Appreciate the range of national, regional, religious and ethnic identities in the United Kingdom. • Think about the lives of people living in other places, and people with different values and customs. • Know that resources can be allocated in different ways and that these economic choices affect individuals, communities and the sustainability of the environment.

What is democracy in education?

As we consider the purpose of education we see democracy embedded within the values of a school. There is an understanding that education includes cognitive development, the intellectual development of knowledge and development of practical skills. Education involves learning how to think and, equally important, develop into a life-long learner (Campbell, 2010). Alongside this sits the development of social skills to enable children to grow into responsible members of society (Mintrom, 2009). Children need to learn about how decisions are made and Grant (2016) suggests this includes making decisions on two levels: as an individual and as an active member of a group. Democracy is an enabling process that helps children to feel empowered because it includes supporting children to take responsibility. Edelstein (2011) refers to democracy as something we need as a life-long learner. Rather than a luxury, it is a basic necessity and it is through educating children that they start to learn about human rights and social inclusion. Democracy in education does not just happen, it takes time for it to grow and develop. Eldelstein (2011) argues that there is no other system than education that provides the right setting because schools involve all children and have a responsibility for preparing children to develop into responsible adults. It is suggested that democracy cannot be learned independently from other aspects of life, but is an integral part of becoming a responsible member of society. A prerequisite to developing democracy comes from dispositions and skills which are needed to be able to engage in sharing and understanding viewpoints, cooperation and taking responsibility for others. This includes learning *about* democracy to make informed choices, learning *through* democracy by being actively involved in making decisions and learning *for* democracy to ensure a sustainable approach for future society (Endelstein, 2011). The involvement of and discussion with parents and children is a critical aspect of fostering democracy in school (Hansen and James, 2015).

Today, as citizens we are constantly being reminded of our democratic right and the important role it plays for us in underpinning a civilised society. However, the notion of democracy can prove a rather complex concept given that it can be interpreted differently in terms of its historic and cultural setting. Furthermore, for children democracy is also a concept that may not be obvious or realised, let alone fully understood by primary-age pupils, given its complex nature. However, what seems important is that it must be seen to be at the heart of a fair and socially equal governing state. As the *Oxford Dictionary* suggests, it is: 'a system of government by the whole population or all the eligible members of a state, typically through elected representatives and the practice or principles of social equality'.

Democracy forms the cornerstone to how our country operates and it is something that we should be proud of. For researchers such as Davies et al. (2002), democracy may be seen to be underpinned by four basic principles – those of: rights, participation, equity and an informed choice. Inseparably linked to the idea of democracy is the idea of freedom of speech and expression. Through this freedom we are able to openly express our ideas and opinions, which may be seen to be developed for the good of all (Universal Declaration of Human Rights (UDHR (1948), Article 19).

For many schools democracy is evident in the way that they and their children live their everyday lives – for example, by the sharing of ideas and opinions in a forum such as a School Council and through the collective decision-making that such a body is involved in. Such activities allow children to cooperatively work together, providing them with real-life experiences of their developing ability to influence and order the decision-making process of schools. As Halstead and Taylor (2000) note, it can also raise children's moral reasoning and levels of understanding about democracy. Through engaging in such issues, as Halstead and Taylor (2000, p.179) go on to note,

> Pupils learned self-governance and found solutions to school problems; they developed skills such as how to conduct meetings, took others' views into account, had consideration for the rights of others and an awareness that their actions could make a difference.

Such a cooperative approach to education, where children learn about the influence of their actions on others and themselves, allies well to seminal researchers on education and democracy such as Dewey (1961). Given the developmental nature of children's education, such an approach would seem vital if, as Rudduck and Flutter (2000, p.86) suggest, 'We should recognise pupils' social maturity and experience by giving them responsibilities and opportunities to share in decision making.'

Through such forms of 'mini-democracy' in schools we can seek to emulate our national system of democracy; children may learn about this concept given that schools themselves are set within their own democratic system of governance. For Gerzon (1997), it is important that if children are to learn about democracy they must not only experience it, but be involved in doing it. By involving children in this democratic process children may also be afforded one of its cornerstone principles – that is, that of freedom of speech and expression whatever their age, something enshrined within Article 12 of the United Convention on the Rights of the Child.

However, nowadays the term 'democracy' has been primarily linked to a school's wish for children to understand the idea of British Values. Such activity is underpinned by schools now having a duty to actively promote the fundamental British Value of democracy as now set out by the government Prevent strategy (HM Government, 2016). For schools and teachers, democracy is also featured in Part

Two of the Teachers' Standards (2012) which states that teachers uphold trust by not undermining fundamental British Values, including democracy. However, despite such recent interest in this notion of democracy it is important that we consider such an exploration of this concept in relation to the long and rich history of our country.

Exploring democracy

For any understanding of democracy it is important to appreciate that this value itself has developed and evolved over time as individuals and collective bodies of people have sought to gain a say in how their country has been and should be run.

The term 'democracy' can be traced back to the ancient Greeks and aligned to a political stance, in which it is related to 'the direct rule of assembled people' (Parry and Moran, 1994, p.3). It was not until the revolutionary era that democracy evolved further from a concept of organisation into a template for societies. One view offered explains that,

> a truly democratic society will be one which permits and perhaps also encourages every man and woman individually or with others to choose the course of his or her life, subject to recognition of the rights of others to do likewise.

Parry and Moran, 1994, p.4

Historically, democracy has, for a long time, been linked to the governance of a country through an elected government which forms part of the parliament. This has not always been the case in our country. Prior to Parliament's establishment and an individual's role and rights in the democratic process being enshrined in law, our country was ruled by the reigning monarch who, under such a feudal system, owned the land and made the laws of the country. However, the first glimmers of our current democracy emerged under King John who, through the Magna Carta, created the principle that individuals could not be imprisoned without a trial. Parliament's embryonic system itself emerged following subsequent meetings of the Great Council of barons and kings under the Norman kings. This, in turn, came to be known as Parliament, with successive rights ceded to parliament such as not allowing interference with its debates and seeking its agreement before the King could create laws. However, it was during the Stuart kings' reigns, the English Civil War and with the Glorious Revolution of 1688 that a constitutional monarchy was established, with Parliament truly able to make its own laws. But, despite the work of movements such as the Chartists (Parliament UK, 2016) and the Suffragettes, it was not until 1928 that both men and women were given equal rights to vote as part of what now may be recognised as our democracy. The voting age was lowered to 18 in 1969. Given such an evolution of our current democratic system, citizens are now all empowered in decision-making and therefore with the ability to make changes to our society. Authors such as Carr and Hartnett (1996) would suggest that a system may be seen in terms of 'contemporary democracy', which now allows concepts such as universal suffrage, centralised leadership and a representative form of government. Within this context, it can be agreed that democracy includes a political stance in which people can have a view and build an argument.

Democracy and the school context

Given democracy's place in our and other countries' history (such as the United States of America), this topic area may include the study of other cultures and people or, through the History National Curriculum, finding out about the importance of significant figures and events in history. A school's curriculum should provide for the spiritual, moral, social and cultural (SMSC) development of children throughout their primary education. Such a focus can be a vehicle to deliver the skills and knowledge necessary to have an understanding of democracy. Additional non-statutory guidance (Department for Education, 2014) also provided for independent, free schools and academies an outline of their obligation regarding SMSC and the delivery of British Values, including democracy. This (Department for Education, 2014, pp.7 and 10) outlines that schools should:

- consider the advantages/disadvantages of democracy;

- understand how democracy and the law works in Britain, in contrast to other forms of government in other countries;

- demonstrate how democracy works by actively promoting democratic processes such as school councils, whose members are voted for by the pupils;

- understand why democracy is perceived in England as the fairest form of political organisation;

- understand why taking part in democracy is a good thing.

It is with their development of citizenship that schools are preparing pupils for their future as active citizens and future members of society. Such work is developed explicitly at Key Stage 3 and 4 through the National Curriculum citizenship programme (Department for Education, 2013). This will include children developing the skills and knowledge to explore social and political issues, as well as exploring how we are governed, democracy and the rule of law. OFSTED (2013) has reported that, for many such schools, citizenship has been integrated via a cross-curricular approach, with subject foci being the vehicle to promote its delivery. Pupil achievement in citizenship was found to be good or better in 28 of 32 primaries; primary schools 'are actively promoting their understanding of democracy and in particular by addressing the idea of citizenship' (OFSTED, 2013, p.5).

Democracy in action: School Council/School Parliament

School councils or in some cases school parliaments can play an important role in the promotion of an understanding of democracy among their pupils. Members of such organisations are encouraged to explore school rules and recognise school practice/resourcing so that a democracy is maintained, in this case within their school. Since the elections of the School Council members are based solely on pupil votes, children can, at first hand, see how our British electoral system works and democracy is upheld in our country. They may also learn that maintaining democracy is not always a smooth and happy journey.

In some school parliaments members are given responsibility for aspects of school life, with roles such as Minister for Health and Fitness; individual class representatives are given the title of Member of Parliament (MP).

By a process of electing representatives from within the class to serve on the Council as its representative, member individuals may take part, first hand, in learning about the procedure of democracy. In some schools hustings are held so that representatives may declare why they are best suited as the class representative. Though sometimes individuals may not be happy with their choice of voted class representative, they can learn that, although they have the right to voice such objections, it is important that the collective, majority decision must be upheld, regardless of individual viewpoints or disapproval. To inform Council discussion, individual pupils are usually allowed regular class debate about whole school issues that they consider in need of change. School Council can also discuss how best, for example, to support the school's charity work throughout the year and the approach taken to events such as Children In Need and Comic Relief.

CASE STUDY: IN THE PLAYGROUND

When it comes to choosing playground equipment using some precious school funds, School Councils are at their peak! One such School Council was 'given' £100 to spend on new resources for the school playground. They had a catalogue and various criteria to guide their spending. The criteria included taking into consideration the small playground space and proximity to the road, health and safety, and the requests of the football players for new footballs. It was amid much excitement that the choosing began. What was interesting to observe was that this School Council, who were predominantly girls, did not seem to contest or deem unfair the request of the footballers. They organised themselves into groups to find and price a range of equipment and then reconvened to discuss and calculate their chosen items. Various pieces of equipment were rejected on the grounds of being too fragile, too large or too expensive. Whilst engaging in an obviously meaningful and very real activity, the level of disinterest in terms of personal gain was remarkable to witness. The group amicably agreed a chosen list that came in within budget and that met with the headteacher's approval, and the shopping list was shared in assembly with the rest of the school, who are now eagerly awaiting their new toys.

KEY QUESTIONS

- What part of these interactions and events can be described as 'democratic'?
- What kind of pre-learning and work must have happened for the children to reach this stage of maturity in their approach?
- What explicit teaching about democracy could have taken place before, during and after this occasion to reinforce understanding of this concept?

The teaching of democracy can also be embedded throughout the life of all schools by the modelling of positive relationships between the children and adults. If adults always take time to listen to children's concerns, pupils will start to understand that it is their right that their individual voice be heard. This can be promoted by the use of circle time. The UK Parliament website produces many other additional support materials for schools to promote the concept of democracy. These include, for example, a link to the Queen in Parliament reading a speech about laws that MPs have made and we have voted for (http://www.parliament.uk/education/teaching-resources-lesson-plans/introduction-to-parliament-ks2-video), as well as ready-made worksheets linked to a debating pack to support school lessons (http://www.parliament.uk/education/teaching-resources-lesson-plans/primary-school-debating-pack/).

CASE STUDY: SCHOOL COUNCIL

Be alert to safeguarding issues arising with this work.

Simon is Headteacher of a primary school in a Midlands town. The school, like so many, has its own School Council, comprised of six pupils (four of whom are girls) who have been democratically elected by their peers from Years 1 to 6 to represent them in this aspect of the school's work. The School Council is voting for

(Continued)

their choice of charity for fundraising support that year. In order to slightly sim-plify the process, Simon has set before the Council just six possible charities to choose from. Each is presented, he believes fairly, and he is sure he has not influ-enced the vote in the way he has talked about the merits of each. Time is getting on and the children are asked to vote. Everyone can see how the others vote, as it is a fairly informal, 'hands-up for this one' approach. The vote goes to an Air Ambulance charity – two of the pupils have had direct experience of this service in their own families and the three others who join this vote are persuaded by their positivity. This leaves one boy, Tom, who did not vote for this charity and who looks visibly disappointed that his wish was not carried. He shrugs and accepts that he did not 'win'. When it comes to organising fundraising activities, however, Tom is not motivated to take part. He happens to be late to the toy sale, set up to raise funds one morning in the playground, and 'forgets' to come to the next School Council meeting.

KEY QUESTIONS

- What valuable learning about democracy in action is there for teachers as well as pupils from this scenario?
- How would you have set up this opportunity for a class or School Council? What would you have done differently from Simon?
- How might Tom's disengagement have been pre-empted and prevented?

This case study scenario rather beautifully, albeit painfully for Tom, exemplifies the frustrations of abiding by a democratic system. An honest and candid look at exam-ples like these, of democracy in action, at pupil level, can help pupils to develop a rounded view of this value, and help introduce the paradox that surrounds apparently straightforward concepts such as this and other values, like fairness, con-sideration and unity.

CASE STUDY: PUPILS 2 PARLIAMENT

Be alert to safeguarding issues arising with this work.

The Year 5 and 6 pupils in a small rural primary school have been invited to take part in a 'Pupils 2 Parliament' discussion. Pupils 2 Parliament is a pro-ject that gives pupils at school a say in decisions being made by Parliament, the Government and other national bodies. It works with schools to help pupils take part in public consultations, when these organisations ask what people think about decisions they are going to make for our country. In this instance, the pupils were given statements about whether the use of microbeads in a range of substances should be banned in law. Roger Morgan, the former Children's Rights Director for England, was in the role as an experienced facilitator for eliciting pupils' ideas and views. The pupils were invited to discuss their views through question scaffolding, which had been carefully crafted in advance of the debate, and which gradually opened and deepened their thinking in this subject, of which they had previously known very little. Knowledge that this was a 'real' debate and that their views would formulate part of a 'real' report to Parliament gave an unparalleled piquancy to this experience. It was notable that pupils of all abilities - including those with educational and health care plans, and those with English as an additional language - all sustained interest throughout. Behaviour was impeccable and the pupils' interest only deepened. However, the most exciting part of the (two-hour) debate was, undoubtedly, the voting. Roger produced three green piggy banks and a bag of plastic voting coins. Everyone was invited to vote for the idea of their choice:

- ban microbeads from all household products;
- do not ban microbeads from household products.

Roger then weighed the pigs on a balance scale and the heaviest one was declared to have carried the vote. The pupils loved this unusual and imaginative method, which demonstrated so clearly how democracy through voting works. Roger told them, because they asked, how voting works in parliament, and they were visibly intrigued by the archaic traditions. This class cannot wait for Roger to return!

KEY QUESTIONS

- What were the merits of this way of introducing democracy to pupils?
- How can a school that does not have access to this project best emulate its effectiveness?

There's nothing like having a real situation such as this one to engage pupils! The House of Commons is serious about engaging young people to get involved in Parliament and UK democracy. Young people are often very passionate about improving their world and invariably have unique and valuable views about how this can happen. Each year, they run a UK Parliament Week to engage pupils across the UK with parliament and, since there is no charge to take part, this is a good option for many schools. However, with so many demands on schools' time, a less effortful way of achieving a similar level of reality can be to set up a School Pupil Parliament and debate national or local issues. Run a mock election to coincide with local elections, explore the Houses of Parliament (you can arrange to take parties for tours or you can go on a virtual tour). Piggy banks like those in the Case Study example are easily procured on the internet! Anything that gives a sense of meaning and helps pupils to feel and see what it is like to really have their views noted is helpful. Invite parents in to see democracy in school at work!

Using real life to exemplify democracy

For schools to make children's understanding of democracy real and relevant they must seize opportunities that present themselves and are linked to this topic. This can include local and general elections, when our local county councillors and MPs are elected. Such events can trigger a real-life situation to study and emulate the democratic process.

CASE STUDY: NEWS CLUB

Be alert to safeguarding issues arising with this work.

Rosa is an experienced teacher. She feels strongly that British Values should be 'meaningful, relevant and demonstrable' for pupils if they are to have any traction in the primary classroom. Her teaching of democracy is best described as incidental. She argues vociferously that it is, nonetheless, possible to demonstrate deep learning of this concept with her Year 6, in whom she has inculcated a vibrant interest in news and current affairs. At her weekly News Club, major national new items are discussed and argued over by the pupils. A recent series of disruptive strikes leads on to an impassioned debate about the right to strike. The pupils grapple with the tensions between individual and group rights and the needs and demands of wider society. One group of pupils declares it is 'mean and unfair' to go on strike and put other people out. The point is made that people get paid to do jobs and they can't 'just decide they're not going to do them'. Someone else draws on a family experience and echoes a family belief that, 'you've got to stick up for yourself because no one else is going to. It's down to you.' No consensus is reached but everyone's viewpoint, argues Rosa, has been a little tested and perhaps expanded.

```
┌──────────────── KEY QUESTIONS ────────────────┐
```

- Is this approach 'enough'? What foundational learning would need to take place for this incidental approach to the teaching of democracy to have that 'traction' that Rosa argued was so critical to sustained thinking and learning?
- What foundational or 'stepped' learning do you see as being necessary through the whole school in order to lead to pupils being capable of this level of analytical thinking?

This kind of engagement with a topic rarely 'just happens'. Much is owed to the individual teacher's proactive and determined mindfulness to keep this method of learning and this approach to thinking alive. Pupils need to build a repertoire of skills in debate and analysis of information, and they need to have had a good grounding in the conventions of debate in order to engage effectively. Many schools choose to adopt an approach to debate through adopting Philosophy for Children and through a secure PSHE and Citizenship curriculum that creates time and space for deep consideration of social and cultural issues. For teachers in schools where this is less well embedded, one way may be to introduce a definition of democracy, and give examples. The pupils would be invited to think of further examples of their own and a working wall of ideas would be constructed. Examples from real and contemporary news could be introduced later as an exemplification. It is highly likely that pupils would be quickly engaged once they perceive relevance to their own lives. Through the Geography curriculum it is possible to link to, 'personal geographies' (Martin, 2005). This involves the teaching of topics that learners can relate to, so that new knowledge builds upon a child's experiences and knowledge. It offers opportunities for pupils to engage in discussion, to question and debate. The basic premise is that children can build upon their knowledge as information, and develop ideas about using their knowledge for understanding which is the foundation for being able to make informed decisions and take informed actions. Although an approach used to teach geography effectively, it can be applied to any subject.

Values into action!

Democracy presents teachers with a challenge: the very fact that we live in a country that operates democracy – and probably have always done so – means that as adults we have perhaps given it scant thought. So, it needs unpicking and illuminating. Democracy is best exemplified in practice, although arguably a certain amount of theoretical background is helpful in supporting teachers to synthesise theory and practice. Arguably, there may be tensions between how we understand democracy in practice and the government's accountability agenda in schools.

Given this, schools may want to work towards developing a programme of study or a cohesive curriculum map to enable this to be addressed in a progressive and developmental way across the school. Here are some suggested strategies that may be part of this whole school approach and/or work as a 'getting started' one-off session:

- starting – or baseline – discussion: what is democracy? Have you ever heard of this value before? What does the dictionary say about it?

- relate to school life: where does democracy play a part? The School Council is an obvious example. What about your class rules? How were they decided? Did you get a say?

- link to the value of fairness;

- present information about countries where there is no democratic system of government. What are the differences you notice? How might you feel if you were living in one of those countries?

- link to history and the suffragette movement; link this to countries where votes for women have only recently been permitted. Explore reasons for this and the effect on men and women of these laws;

- link to maths: challenge each child or group to count how many times in a day they experience democracy at work, in the playground when choosing people to play a game, in the classroom when discussing who should go first etc.;

- homework challenge: interview your parents and siblings about where they see democracy happening at home;

- share a Powerpoint™ or similar about democracy, outlining what it is, why we have it and what difference it makes to our lives. Show footage of the Houses of Parliament and law courts;

- challenge the class to make a pamphlet for parents about 'the value of democracy in Britain';

- make a class or personal presentation for assembly, or for a public speaking event; invite parents and record it so that their involvement is maximised;

- invite your local MP to come and talk about democracy at work;

- research how other countries organise their political systems, in particular those who are not known as democratic states: how do they differ from our own and why might this be?

- start to map them into the curriculum: create a specific place in planning formats to ensure that links are made;

- ensure specific attention is paid to safeguarding opportunities, such as knowing that these universal rights are there to protect everyone and have primacy both over national law and family and community practices;

- carry out an audit: how and where can this British Value link into other areas of the curriculum?

- involve pupils in creating a school display to exemplify this British Value;

- older pupils will begin to be able to consider the limitations/possible frustrations presented by the value of democracy. See Case Study below.

Other activities that can promote an understanding of democracy might include the following:

- each class drawing up their class rules at the beginning of the year and the rights and responsibilities associated with these rules;

- when the class is provided with a budget by the school to spend on their classroom and its resourcing;

- class-based topics such as ancient Greece, the Romans or the Victorians;

- voting for other forms of school representatives such as school buddies, eco-warriors, digital leaders, house/sports captains.

A SUMMARY OF KEY POINTS FROM THIS CHAPTER

- Schools have a statutory duty to teach pupils about British Values in a way that is commensurate with the age and ability of its pupils, regardless of its context.
- Schools can draw on resources for schools from the House of Commons and local MPs.

(Continued)

- Democracy is a key British Value, linked to citizenship and PSHE, as well as the Prevent agenda.

- Pedagogy is all-important in teaching about democracy for British Values: it needs to be meaningful, relevant and fun.

- The teaching of all British Values, including democracy, must support pupils with learning difficulties and wellbeing needs.

- Effective teaching involves working with parents.

- The school needs to support pupils using a developmental and progressive curriculum approach.

- Schools may wish to seek outside support from other agencies to promote this teaching and learning.

- Schools must be mindful of safeguarding issues in relation to teaching about this area of British Values, and must be cognisant of their duties to report any suspected radicalisation.

References

Campbell, J.M. (2010) 'Importance of rule of law to civil society'. *Defense Counsel Journal*, 77 (3): 287–8.

Carr, W. and Hartnett, A. (1996) *Education and the Struggle for Democracy*. Buckingham: Open University Press.

Catling, S. and Martin, F. (n.d.) Contesting *powerful knowledge*: the primary geography curriculum as an articulation between academic and children's (ethno-) geographies Available at: https://ore.exeter.ac.uk/repository/bitstream/handle/10871/9741/Curric%20Journal%20-Contesting%20powerful%20knowledge.pdf?sequence Contesting *powerful knowledge*: The primary geography curriculum as an articulation between academic and children's (ethno-) geographies =2%20 (accessed 3 April 2017).

Davies, L., Harber, C. and Schweisfurth, M. (2002) *Democracy through Teacher Education: A Guide Book for Use with Students Teachers*. Birmingham: CIER.

Department for Education (2012) Teachers' Standards. DFE-00066-2011. London: Department for Education.

Department for Education (2013) Citizenship programmes of study: key stages 3 and 4. National Curriculum in England. Available at: https://www.gov.uk/government/uploads/system/uploads/attachment_data/file/239060/SECONDARY_national_curriculum_-_Citizenship.pdf (accessed 10 March 2017).

Department for Education (2014) Improving the spiritual, moral, social and cultural (SMSC) development of pupils: supplementary guidance. Available at: https://www.gov.uk/government/uploads/system/uploads/attachment_data/file/380396/Improving_the_spiritual__moral__social_and_cultural__SMSC__development_of_pupils_supplementary_information.pdf (accessed 10 July 2017).

Dewey, J. (1961) *Democracy and Education:* An Introduction to the Philosophy of Education. New York: Macmillan.

Edelstein, W. (2011) 'Education for democracy: reasons and strategies'. *European Journal of Education*, 46 (1): 127–37.

Gerzon, M. (1997) 'Teaching democracy by doing it!'. *Educational Leadership*, 54 (5): 6–11.

Grant, C. (2016) 'Voices, not numbers: towards a greater democracy in education'. *Monthly Review: An Independent Socialist Magazine*, 68 (1): 35–41.

Halstead, M.J. and Taylor, M. (2000) 'Learning and teaching about values: a review of recent research'. *Cambridge Journal of Education*, (30) 2: 169–202.

Hansen, D.T. and James, C. (2015) 'The importance of cultivating democratic habits in schools: enduring lessons from *Democracy and Education*'. *Journal of Curriculum Studies*, 48 (1): 94–112.

HM Government (2016) Revised *Prevent* Duty Guidance: For England and Wales. Available at: https://www.gov.uk/government/uploads/system/uploads/attachment_data/file/445977/3799_Revised_Prevent_Duty_Guidance__England_Wales_V2-Interactive.pdf (accessed 2 March 2016).

Martin, F. (2005) 'Photographs don't speak'. *Primary Geographer*, Spring: 7–11.

Mintrom, M. (2009) 'Promoting local democracy in education: challenges and prospects'. *Educational Policy*, 23 (2): 329–54.

OFSTED (2013) Citizenship consolidated? Available at: https://www.gov.uk/government/publications/citizenship-consolidated-a-survey-of-citizenship-in-schools (accessed 7 March 2017).

Parliament UK (2016) Chartists. Available at http://www.parliament.uk/about/living-heritage/transformingsociety/electionsvoting/chartists/overview/chartistmovement/ (accessed 2 March 2017).

Parry, G. and Moran, M. (1994) *Democracy and Democratization*. London: Routledge.

Rudduck, J. and Flutter, J. (2000) 'Pupil participation and pupil perspective: "carving a new experience of education"'. *Cambridge Journal of Education*, 31 (1): 75–89.

Teacher resources and lesson plans. Available at: http://www.parliament.uk/education/teaching-resources-lesson-plans?cat=lawmaking (accessed 11 December 2017).

3
INDIVIDUAL LIBERTY

This chapter explores:

- the definition of individual liberty in Britain as part of the British Values requirements and in relation to the Prevent programme;
- the importance of a whole school approach to teaching about individual liberty in the primary school;
- the relationship between safeguarding and the delivery of the concept of individual liberty in Britain as part of the British Values requirements and in relation to the Prevent programme;
- strategies that promote the effective delivery of the concept of individual liberty in Britain as part of the British Values requirements.

Teachers' Standards

This chapter supports the development of the following Teachers' Standards:

TS1: Set high expectations which inspire, motivate and challenge pupils:

- a safe and stimulating environment for pupils, rooted in mutual respect;
- set goals that stretch and challenge pupils of all backgrounds, abilities and dispositions.

TS7: Manage behaviour effectively to ensure a good and safe learning environment:

- manage classes effectively, using approaches which are appropriate to pupils' needs in order to involve and motivate them.

Part Two: Personal and professional conduct

Teachers uphold public trust in the profession and maintain high standards of ethics and behaviour, within and outside school, by:

- treating pupils with dignity, building relationships rooted in mutual respect, and at all times observing proper boundaries appropriate to a teacher's professional position;

- not undermining fundamental British Values, including democracy, the rule of law, individual liberty and mutual respect, and tolerance of those with different faiths and beliefs;

- ensuring that personal beliefs are not expressed in ways which exploit pupils' vulnerability or might lead them to break the law.

Introduction

This chapter will focus on defining liberty, as well as examining the role it can play in aspects of our daily lives in schools. Furthermore, this chapter will seek to examine the notion of liberty and how such a concept is understood by pupils. It will also examine strategies for the successful integration of this concept within a whole school approach to promoting British Values.

The relationship between the National Curriculum and British Values: individual liberty

Table 3.1 Links to the National Curriculum: individual liberty

PSHE Key Stage 1	<ul><li>Know about Children's Rights and Human Rights.</li><li>Share opinions on things that matter to them and explain their views through discussions.</li><li>Listen to other people and play and work cooperatively (including strategies to resolve simple arguments through negotiation).</li><li>Recognise what they like and dislike, how to make real, informed choices that improve their physical and emotional health.</li><li>Recognise that choices can have good and not so good consequences.</li><li>Recognise what is fair and unfair, kind and unkind, what is right and wrong.</li><li>Recognise when people are being unkind either to them or others.</li></ul>

PSHE Key Stage 2	• Know how to make informed choices (including recognising that choices can have positive, neutral and negative consequences) and to begin to understand the concept of a 'balanced lifestyle'. • Research, discuss and debate topical issues, problems and events concerning health and wellbeing and offer their recommendations to appropriate people. • Recognise that they may experience conflicting emotions and when they might need to listen to their emotions or overcome them. • Understand that everyone has human rights, all peoples and all societies, and that children have their own special rights set out in the United Nations Declaration of the Rights of the Child. • Recognise that they share a responsibility for keeping themselves and others safe, when to say, 'yes', 'no', 'I'll ask' and 'I'll tell'. • Know that these universal rights are there to protect everyone and have primacy both over national law and family and community practices. • Realise the consequences of anti-social and aggressive behaviours such as bullying and discrimination of individuals and communities. • Know that there are different kinds of responsibilities, rights and duties at home, at school, in the community and towards the environment. • Resolve differences by looking at alternatives, seeing and respecting others' points of view, making decisions and explaining choices. • Appreciate the range of national, regional, religious and ethnic identities in the United Kingdom.
Religious education	• The need to respect the right of all individuals to practise their own faith or to reject a faith system.
Science	• The place of individual liberty in the construct of hypotheses and conclusions.
History	• KS1: *Lives of Significant Individuals*: Rosa Parks and Emily Davison. • British resistance, for example, Boudica.
Geography	• Equip pupils with knowledge about diversity.
Languages	• The ability to converse in another language (and to think in another language) leading to the ability to connect with others beyond our cultural and geographical borders.
Design and technology	• The role of individual liberty in the creative process, enabling us to design, make and evaluate a range of products.
Art	• The role of individual liberty to be experimental and innovative in the creative process, enabling the creation of new shapes, forms and images in a variety of media.

What is Liberty?

In the past, ideas about Britishness have been less explicit in United Kingdom (UK) education than in many other Western nations. Kerr (1999) suggests this is due to an understanding by everyone about what British identity was. More recently, Tomlinson (2008) recognises how the discourse of Britishness has evolved from the 1950s into the 1960s through integration moving on to multi-culturalism from the 1970s. Previously, it is clear that there has been no reference to terrorism; it is since the recent attacks that discussions now centre upon developing a shared understanding of British Values. Within the current debate is a need to recognise how to promote the value of liberty. Yet the concept of liberty, linked to British Values, is arguably one of the most difficult to teach and define with adults, young people and children. Importantly, it must be seen to have no boundaries in terms of its reach in order to do good in our society. Liberty has been open to different interpretations, having different meanings in different contexts, and has changed over time (Richardson, 2015). Current debates provide a reminder that liberty is a value shared by many societies and is not exclusive to British society. Currently, there is a need to agree and recognise liberty as a value. Teachers need to show a commitment to pupils in school, to give them the space and time to discuss their understanding and share their beliefs about liberty. This opens up a safe environment in which pupils can express themselves and talk openly (Elton-Chalcraft et al., 2017).

As individuals who value our liberty and freedom we are constantly being reminded through the media of how those less fortunate than ourselves can be oppressed, not only in terms of their freedom of expression with regard to their free thinking, but also in terms of their actions in society, often linked to their governance. However, the notion of liberty can prove a rather complex concept for children as it may not be obvious or realised, let alone fully understood, given that such liberty is enshrined as part of their daily lives. But, as the *Cambridge Dictionary* (2017) suggests, the significance of liberty is that it is: 'the freedom to live as you wish or go where you want'.

For many individuals the notion of freedom is synonymous with the idea of liberty. However, it is important to realise that freedom allows individuals to make decisions without any controls being exerted in terms of external requirements or pressure, whereas liberty involves freedom being permitted by those who govern – that is, the right to do what an individual wishes within the law. Liberty, therefore, should be seen in terms of being free with the constraint of being under a legal context. People, by their very nature, are meant to live in freedom;

however, it is the government of society that will grant such liberty to its people. Governments, therefore, do their utmost, with regards to laws and action, to secure such freedoms so that liberty may be exercised by all. This requires not only a moral, but also an ethical approach to the law and, most importantly, the appointment of a government and leaders who are there not for personal gain but with a secure understanding of the huge responsibilities that they hold to be democratic.

For many schools the granting of freedom through children's liberty may be seen to be evident in the way that children freely live their everyday lives. OFSTED (2015) would suggest that such a focus may be found in terms of schools and their leaders supporting pupils' spiritual, moral, social and cultural (SMSC) development. This will, therefore, allow children to: 'demonstrate skills and attitudes that will allow them to participate fully in and contribute positively to life in modern Britain' (OFSTED, 2015, p.35).

As teachers we are reminded of a public and social responsibility towards helping pupils to promote British Values, British law and discourage adherence to religious law where it conflicts with the law of the land (Department for Education, 2014a). Such freedoms of children's liberty are vital since, as Fisher (2002) notes, independent children, who possess the skill to think critically, who can self-govern their own thinking and beliefs, are crucial to classroom and future life. Practices such as school councils provide a means to support an individual's sense of belonging to a community. Such practices have strong links to the ongoing educational agenda of providing opportunities to promote pupils' participation and to allow their 'voice' to be heard and their views harnessed to provide positive outcomes for their schools (Rudduck and Flutter, 2004). School councils allow children to work cooperatively together, providing them with real-life experiences of their ability to act freely so as to develop and to influence the decision-making process of schools. Furthermore, such practices allow individuals an opportunity to sense what it feels like to be part of a democratic process where they have been elected to represent others, with the freedom to speak on their behalf. This model allows the pupils to have a say in the running and organisation of the school – for example, by the sharing of ideas in a School Council meeting – without fear of criticism or sanction if their views do not support those of the headteacher. The National College of School Leadership (NCSL) clearly supports this notion and such associated practices by noting it is by actively being engaged in the decision-making linked to the life of the school that children have the ability to learn and apply those very skills that can promote them as active citizens in the wider world (Johnson, 2004).

Exploring liberty

Along with all the British Values, liberty as a concept is inextricably linked to the ideals of both individual and collective freedom of thought and actions. This is understood as the tolerance exerted by the law linked to religious, ethical and moral considerations. The ideal of promoting and defining liberty has ebbed and flowed throughout history with such a struggle continuing in society today across the world. Historical milestones such as Magna Carta (1215) have made significant inroads into recognising the notion of freedom under the rule of law. As such it often forms a fundamental place in the ideals of English liberty by establishing the right to a trial, and appeal against imprisonment without a trial. The Magna Carta also acknowledged that no one should be seen to be above the law. Activist groups such as the Levellers in 1647 called for equality in the law and in liberty of conscience when considering matters of religion, with early seminal authors such as John Locke seeking to challenge and promote the view that government should be obliged morally to protect people's life, liberty and property (Powell, 2000). Such freedom to promote liberty has led to many breakthroughs with regard to how people are treated in society. Acts such as the 1833 Slavery Abolition Act outlawing the slave trade throughout the British Empire and the 1948 Declaration of Human Rights have gone a long way to enshrine liberty as a freedom for society's people. Nowadays such a drive to promote the idea of liberty may be seen in terms of how such human rights cover gender, race and religion, with the Human Rights Act 1998 now ensuring that everyone should be treated not only fairly, but with dignity.

Linked, in particular, to promoting children's freedom of liberty is the UN Convention on Children's Rights (UNCRC) (UNICEF, 2017). It seeks to explore how adults and governments alike can promote all children's rights by establishing the economic, political, social, civil and cultural rights that they should be entitled to. This convention includes Articles such as 12 and 14 to make certain that a child's voice is heard and such expression or opinion should be freely made. Given such freedom of liberty it now seems that young people have an increased awareness of and engagement with issues that will affect them. This, in turn, has meant that children are much more involved in the society in which they live. For example, in many schools the promotion of a green agenda linked to the ideals of sustainability has led to children being key contributors to eco-committees to support such an initiative both in their schools and the local environments. Given such a drive to encourage liberty, it is fundamentally important that schools and teachers promote the ideal that liberty may not just be seen by one's actions in society, but also that individuals have the right to make socially acceptable choices – and, to do that, you need to be able to respect and distinguish between right and wrong in relationship to civil and criminal law. As teachers, it is also your role to prepare children and to help them develop an understanding and appreciation of the diversity of our country so that they may challenge stereotypical views and opinions that may be prevalent (Lander, 2016).

The rise of globalisation and children's access to social media and the news relating to political, social and humanitarian struggles for liberty have meant that such situations are real and meaningful to children. They are very much at the centre of a global age. This has resulted in children who are keen to understand and discuss such issues in terms of what is socially acceptable or not in our wider society today. They are keen to support such struggles through organised charitable work – for example, Comic Relief and the Red Cross. Through all such levels of engagement, the ideals of freedom of liberty may be explored by children so that they can be involved in the full democratic process and be educated about their rights to grow up to be free and active citizens who can make a difference. The government guidance encourages headteachers to engage keenly with British law, although it is suggested that there is a need to accommodate differences too, which includes differences between people and cultures alongside promoting British Values. The assumption is that teachers will have the knowledge and the confidence to promote and uphold British Values. A challenge remains in how teachers are supported to meet the government agenda and provide a balanced perspective.

Teaching and learning and liberty

The curriculum can provide a rich medium to plan for and to explore the notion of liberty as part of class-based teaching and learning. However, it is important that both the school and you as a class teacher map opportunities to promote the teaching of the value of liberty in the curriculum so that vital learning opportunities are not missed. Perhaps it may be a good idea to create a specific place in your current planning formats to ensure that such links are made.

Subjects such as history can provide obvious clear and tangible links to how, over time, our civil liberties have been championed both in this country and abroad – for example, the abolition of slavery, aspects of persecution in the Second World War linked to the Jews and studies of apartheid and American civil liberties struggles linked to race. This can help children to gain a better understanding of how liberty has been fought for and how the withdrawal of such a value can have dire consequences for those involved. Subjects such as geography can allow for the global political appreciation of areas of the world that struggle to support – or even acknowledge the value of liberty. Through this subject children may start to appreciate areas of the world where liberty may fail to flourish or even be suppressed due to a fear of brutal dictatorships. Thus, by using such areas of the curriculum, teachers may share with pupils an understanding of countries where people's freedoms of liberty are restricted. What are the differences that pupils notice? How might children feel if you were living in one of those countries? Study of the Religious Education curriculum can also allow for an understanding of the freedom of religious expression, tolerance, diversity and the law, which is underpinned by an expression of liberty.

As well as being driven by aspects of the curriculum, liberty can be linked to the school's personal, health, social and citizenship education (PHSCE). Through practices such as circle time, attention to social emotional aspects of learning (SEAL), visiting speakers and role play, discussion and understanding of this value may be developed. As Weare (2015) and the PSHE Association (2015) suggest, for learning to be effective it is essential to provide good problem-solving skills. PSHE (2015) suggest that personal, social and health education (PHSE) can help provide children with the skills, knowledge, understanding and language that will enable them to adopt healthy thoughts, behaviours and strategies.

Many opportunities exist that can lead to chances to explore children's widening awareness of the national and international ideals of liberty linked to liberty – even from an early age, as this case study shows.

CASE STUDY: THE CONCEPT OF SLAVERY

Be alert to safeguarding issues arising with this work.

A mixed Year 1 and 2 class are discussing *Farmer Duck* by Martin Waddell and Helen Oxenbury as part of their English focus on recount writing. The children are aghast at the duck's treatment by the fat and lazy farmer; they quickly form an allegiance with the put-upon duck. Their teacher introduces the concept of slavery. Some of the children have heard this term and know what it means. One or two can say a little about slavery of 'black people in chains and it was really bad'. None of the children know about modern-day slavery and are wide-eyed at this prospect. The teacher does not dwell on this concept for fear of frightening so young a class, but nevertheless pursues the idea tentatively. A discussion ensues.

KEY QUESTIONS

- This is an opportunistic means of addressing this key British Value of Liberty. What role do such opportunities play in a school's whole approach to teaching about key British Values?
- In this instance, the teacher left the unplanned discussion as unrecorded – should/could she have found a way of using this as either evidence of coverage

> or even of assessment of British Values? How could she share this with colleagues across the school?
>
> - Does this unsought happening point to a new way forward? Could a story-based approach be the way forward for teaching British Values in primary schools?
>
> - What are the potential safeguarding issues here?

These 'surprise' opportunities for deepening and developing pupils' understanding of British Values are common, and seem to grow increasingly so as teacher awareness increases. Stories can have a powerful place to play in a child's understanding of life and its dilemmas. For children they can also form a means by which to identify sometimes quite powerful emotions which link to the issue in hand. As schools and teachers become more and more familiar with British Values they will increasingly be able to map a meaningful cross-curricular approach to their teaching, using stories as a means to promote discussion and encourage empathy with the chosen focus. As ad hoc situations arise, they can have a key value in helping pupils connect theory and reality, but, arguably, they have more value when really capitalised on. Many teachers are reluctant, these days, to go 'off piste' when the curriculum is already so crowded, but there would have been opportunities here to, for example, set research as homework to find out more about slavery – both in the past and the present, to have a wider philosophical discussion about this issue and to encourage children to record their findings and responses as part of a display or class book. All such work will have a key part to play in promoting the social, moral and cultural development of the child. This story was an opportunity with more potential to be wrung from it. In terms of safeguarding, this subject area has the potential to invite disclosures. Some children may be aware of the lives of people who are being unfairly treated or exploited in their own families. All teachers must have due regard for the safeguarding implications and act in accordance with school policy if anything arises.

Liberty in school life

The notion of liberty connects very well with a desire to encourage pupils to see the link between understanding and accepting individual responsibility for their behaviour in school and in life in general. Children are taught that schools are a safe place and that they should not only ask questions but challenge issues that they feel are unjust in a respectful manner. They are encouraged to see that, regardless of school rules, individual liberty should not be suppressed. One such major policy that encapsulates such a drive to promote freedom and order is that of the school's behaviour policy. Such a document is a governmental requirement (Department for Education, 2012a) and it serves to outline the behaviour expected in schools, alongside the rewards and sanctions that will be meted out as a result of children's actions.

The whole school behaviour policy forms one of the cornerstones of schools' attempts to help children see how their individual freedom of liberty should be not be inhibited is the school's work and rules relating to prohibiting bullying. Such ideals to promote children's safety are shared by the current inspection regime, OFSTED, when judging the quality of a school's leadership and management. OFSTED (2015, p.51) is concerned with how well a school provision contributes not only to the physical safety of children and young people, but also to their 'emotional health, safety and wellbeing'. You can encourage pupils to think about the rights of every child to live a life without harassment or abuse. Explore feelings children may experience when alienated from their peers because they need to express their individual needs and rights using books such as *Bill's New Frock*, by Anne Fine, about a boy who has to experience what it is like to be a girl, *The Boy in the Striped Pyjamas* by John Boyne or watch carefully selected clips from the film *Billy Elliot* about a child who succeeds in becoming a dancer in spite of parental and cultural opposition. Children need to realise that their freedom of choice and actions will be linked to consequences, which may impact upon a child's personal liberty in school.

The following case study exemplifies this quite starkly.

CASE STUDY: LIBERTY AND THE BOUNDARIES OF SCHOOL AUTHORITY

Be alert to safeguarding issues arising with this work.

A Year 6 boy, in the spring term of his final year of primary school, is well aware of the approaching transition to high school. Throughout his school life he has struggled, off and on, with abiding by the school's rules and he has constantly challenged the boundaries of school authority. Although bright for his age, he finds application to his school work hard and struggles to see the point of being at school. He has been actively encouraged to make positive choices, knowing that he is in a safe and supportive environment. Despite the school constantly working with him to see that he must control his actions, and his being given an exclusion warning for unusually intimidating and unacceptable behaviour to his peers, he initiates a systematic and ongoing set of intimidating actions towards a boy in his class and this act leads to a half-day exclusion - this is his first exclusion. Reflecting on his behaviour later on, he says, 'I can't believe what I did. They were my friends.'

KEY QUESTIONS

- How might this case be seen to be linked to the notion of liberty?
- What sort of advice would you give to this pupil in terms of helping him understand the difference between his own personal freedom to act the way he wishes and the impact it may have on liberty?
- What role, if any, do happenings like these play in a school's whole approach to teaching about key individual liberty?

This is a fairly typical example of what happens in an organisation when individual liberty conflicts with the rights of others. The boy may have felt he was not doing anything that was particularly wrong at the time and that his actions were justified; however, despite his feeling, he must see that his actions had consequences. For him, the price was his own personal liberty. He needs to be made aware: that his actions have undermined not only his own personal rights and freedoms, but also those of his victims; that bullying will not be tolerated in any form in school and society as a whole. This boy needs to be helped to be more self-reflective so that he can have greater empathy with how his actions have made others now feel and act. Some sort of peer mediation may help both the bully and bullied come to terms with what has gone on. The boy needs to be helped to find ways to show contrition to his victim so that that individual does not live in fear of this happening again. The bully needs to see that he was in the wrong and that he has broken the school behaviour policy. This could have been a supreme opportunity, with the boy's permission, to use a very real example for discussion with the older classes about the place of individual liberty in a school setting and how actions can suppress such a value.

Promoting teaching about the value of liberty

Individual liberty may sometimes be seen as an 'invisible' value. We are rarely fully conscious that in Britain we have a way of life that contains considerable liberty, compared to some countries. Importantly, this liberty has its limits. Therefore, the exploration of this value is the most nuanced of them all, providing an opportunity to evoke deep thinking and philosophical reasoning. When you are working with children you will realise that they can engage in many activities to develop an active role in promoting an understanding of liberty: for example, sharing their view with school managers such as the headteacher, the governors and people in the public eye such as an MP. All such work encourages individuals to explore their views on the world and to make informed choices about their actions. However, for some children such an exploration of liberty comes with aspects of internal conflict, which may take empathy and intelligence to reconcile. For example, all children have differing needs which often will result in an individualised approach to the way they are educated in schools – such as children with autistic traits, whose differences from their peers in the way they act may mean that a whole school approach and response to their individual liberties and freedoms might raise particular issues. Though schools may wish to treat children equally and with the same level of concern it will not always mean that they can be treated in an exactly similar manner. Flexibility will be the key so that rules and boundaries may be reinterpreted and intelligently applied. Importantly, children should be helped to see why such variance is needed; however, justice will be upheld.

Class-based organisational systems such as zone boards and 'golden time' in schools may form a tangible means by which freedom of liberty can be explored and linked to the idea of their behaviour in class. Practices such as golden time also give the child access to the democratic process by the establishment of agreed golden rules, such as being honest and looking after property. These underpin acceptable behaviour in a classroom and school by providing a set boundaries to the freedoms linked to that of personal liberty. Golden time can allow children to start to realise that they have the freedom to choose and to select their reward for good behaviour. It provides a means to allow the school to help the children to discover the notion of freedom of choice linked to actions, and the impact their actions can have on future liberty.

We could be led to believe that many adults will not have given the concept of liberty as much thought as you are about to do with your pupils, so it is important that your school has a whole school shared understanding of what liberty means in your school. Start any work you propose by having a baseline agreement among your colleagues of:

- What does the concept of 'liberty' mean to you, your class and the school?

- What are you currently doing to support this value and what can be done to promote this value further?

- What do pupils see this value to mean and how is it supported by the school's practice?

- What liberties do you and the children enjoy in school life?

Values into action!

Sometimes when you are considering promoting the value of liberty it may be best approached through looking at the opposite of this value – that is, subjugation or constraint. You may also like to ask pupils to consider what unrestricted liberty may be like in our world or a school and how this could lead to potential chaos. Start by giving children a real-life scenario to consider – for example, if your parents said you could go to bed or go anywhere at any time, what might be the result of this? Other suggestions that may help promote this value include:

- consider a 'live' or topical issue – for example, some schools have banned the 'large hair ribbon', a craze that was started by a schoolgirl in the US under the banner of individual liberty. More seriously, some schools have tried to ban the wearing of the hijab by female students. What impact could these restrictions have on individual liberty? Should a ban like this have merit?

- challenge the older pupils in the school to write a creative story about this value to share with younger pupils. They may wish to include a moral message about the importance of speaking out;

- talk about the need for bravery, courage and independence of thought when expressing opinions linked to liberty, which may include unusual ideas – and how this can be part of individual liberty (as long as we do not, in expressing them, contravene laws about unduly offending individuals or groups of people, or incite violence). Make outline reference to the laws of slander here – people may not say things that are slanderous or endanger people through falsehoods;

- gradually exemplify the links between this and other British Values, which have many things in common with the value of democracy and with the human value of responsibility;

- ensure specific attention is paid to safeguarding opportunities, such as knowing that these universal rights are there to protect everyone and have primacy both over national law and family and community practices;

- what children's stories present possibilities for an entry point to this topic or for discussing it further?

- invite pupils to create a PDF or similar to exemplify how this British Value impacts on their lives at school to display on the school website;

- you may even like to venture into the territory of how money links to liberty, with older pupils by exploring: how does money come into it? Where and in what ways can money buy you freedoms you might not otherwise enjoy? This is a sensitive and possibly uncomfortable arena – but just consider the preponderance of opportunities now, for example, to upgrade your flight by buying privileged boarding and greater legroom on the plane, or to buy more expensive tickets at the theatre to guarantee you a better view. How do people make choices with their money to buy them greater freedoms?

A SUMMARY OF KEY POINTS FROM THIS CHAPTER

- There has been and still continues to be a struggle to establish the value of liberty for all.
- With liberty comes responsibility for one's actions.
- Engaging in the value of liberty, children can develop critical thinking skills to become a valued part of their school and the community.
- The value of liberty can be practised in schools by allowing children to share their views on whatever concerns or troubles them, whilst allowing them to see that such liberty can change things.
- Schools can make direct links with the value of liberty to the National Curriculum and its requirements. These can be made explicit with pupils and serve to teach and reinforce the value.
- Teachers need to be alert to where the concept can arise unexpectedly and maximise these opportunities whilst being mindful of safeguarding issues.
- This value necessarily leads us into the territory of anti-bullying, tolerance of individual faith and culture – and therefore has a direct relationship with the Prevent strategy.
- The values of liberty are wide-ranging and will lead you to consider such issues as race, faith, culture and gender.
- Schools must be mindful of safeguarding issues in relation to teaching about this area of British Values, and must be cognisant of their duties to report any suspected radicalisation.

References

Cambridge Dictionary (2017) Available at http://dictionary.cambridge.org/dictionary/english/liberty (accessed 1 July 2017).

Department for Education (2012a) Ensuring Good Behaviour in schools: a summary for head teachers, governing bodies, teachers. Available at: https://www.gov.uk/government/publications/behaviour-and-discipline-in-schools (accessed 30 May 2017).

Department for Education (2012b) Teachers' Standards. DFE-00066-2011. London: Department for Education.

Department for Education (2014a) *Promoting Fundamental British Values in Social Moral, Spiritual and Cultural Education in Schools*. London: Department for Education.

Department for Education (2014b) The National Curriculum in England. Available at: https://www.gov.uk/government/publications/national-curriculum-in-england-frame work-for-key-stages-1-to-4 (accessed 14 October 2016).

Elton-Chalcraft, S., Linder, V., Revell, L., Warner, D. and Whitworth, L. (2017) 'To promote, or not to promote fundamental British Values? Teachers' Standards, diversity and teacher education'. *British Educational Research Journal*, 43 (1): 29–48.

Fisher, J. (2002) *Starting from the Child*. 2nd edn. Maidenhead: Open University Press.

Johnson, K. (2004) Children's Voices. Available at: http://dera.ioe.ac.uk/5067/1/randd-pupil-lship-johnson.pdf (accessed 1 June 2017).

Kerr, D. (1999) *Citizenship Education: An International Comparison*. London: QCA.

Lander, V. (2016) 'Introduction to fundamental British Values'. *Journal of Education for Teaching*, 42 (3): 274–9.

Maylor, U. (2016) 'I'd worry about how to teach it': British Values in English classrooms. *Journal of Education for Teaching*, 42 (3): 314–8.

OFSTED (2015) School inspection handbook: handbook for inspecting schools in England under section 5 of the Education Act 2005. Available at: https://www.gov.uk/government/publications/school-inspection-handbook-from-september-2015 (accessed 12 November 2016).

Powell, J. (2000) Life, Liberty, and Property: A Biography of John Locke. Available at: https://www.libertarianism.org/publications/essays/life-liberty-property-biography-john-locke (accessed 24 May 2017).

PSHE Association (2015) Teacher guidance: preparing to teach about mental health and emotional wellbeing. Available at: https://www.selfinjurysupport.org.uk/docfiles/PSHE-Association-Preparing-To-Teach-About-Emotional-Health-and-Wellbeing.pdf (accessed 27 April 2017).

Richardson, R. (2015) 'British Values and British identity'. *London Review of Education*, 13 (2):37–48.

Rudduck, J. and Flutter, J. (2004) *Consulting Pupils: What's in it for Schools?* London: RoutledgeFalmer.

Tomlinson, S. (2008) *Race and Education: Policy and Politics in Education*. Maidenhead: Open University Press.

UNICEF (2017) How we protect children's rights with the UN convention on the rights of the child. Available at: https://www.unicef.org.uk/what-we-do/un-convention-child-rights/ (accessed 31 May 2017).

Weare, K. (2015) *What Works in Promoting Social and Emotional Well-being and Responding to Mental Health Problems in School?* London: National Children's Bureau.

Further reading

Mailes, H. and Deuchar, R. (2006) '"We don't learn democracy, we live it!" Consulting the pupil voice in Scottish schools'. *Education, Citizenship and Social Justice*, 1 (3): 249–66.

Parliament UK (2017) Civil liberties and personal freedoms – discussion activity. Available at: http://www.parliament.uk/education/teaching-resources-lesson-plans?cat=lawmaking (accessed 12 December 2017).

4
THE RULE OF LAW

This chapter explores:

- the definition of the rule of law in Britain as part of the British Values requirements and in relation to the Prevent programme;
- the importance of a differentiated approach to teaching about the rule of law in the primary school;
- the relationship between safeguarding and the delivery of the rule of law in Britain as part of the British Values requirements and in relation to the Prevent programme;
- strategies that promote the effective delivery of the rule of law in Britain as part of the British Values requirements.

Teachers' Standards

This chapter supports the development of the following Teachers' Standards:

TS1: Set high expectations which inspire, motivate and challenge pupils:

- a safe and stimulating environment for pupils, rooted in mutual respect.

TS7: Manage behaviour effectively to ensure a good and safe learning environment:

- maintain good relationships with pupils, exercise appropriate authority and act decisively when necessary.

Part Two: Personal and professional conduct

Teachers uphold public trust in the profession and maintain high standards of ethics and behaviour, within and outside school, by:

- treating pupils with dignity, building relationships rooted in mutual respect, and at all times observing proper boundaries appropriate to a teacher's professional position;

- not undermining fundamental British Values, including democracy, the rule of law, individual liberty and mutual respect, and tolerance of those with different faiths and beliefs;

- ensuring that personal beliefs are not expressed in ways which exploit pupils' vulnerability or might lead them to break the law.

The relationship between the National Curriculum and British Values: the rule of law

Although personal, social and health education (PSHE), including citizenship, is not currently a compulsory part of the National Curriculum, many teachers would argue that this subject is a vital component of any child's education.

Table 4.1 Curriculum links

PSHE Key Stage 1	<ul><li>Know that they belong to various groups and communities such as family and school.</li><li>Know about Children's Rights and Human Rights.</li><li>Share opinions on things that matter to them and explain their views through discussions.</li><li>Listen to other people and play and work cooperatively (including strategies to resolve simple arguments through negotiation).</li><li>Judge what kind of physical contact is acceptable, comfortable, unacceptable and uncomfortable and how to respond (including whom to tell and how to tell them).</li><li>Recognise when people are being unkind either to them or others, how to respond, whom to tell and what to say.</li><li>Know that there are different types of teasing and bullying, that these are wrong and unacceptable.</li><li>Know how to resist teasing or bullying, if they experience or witness it, whom to go to and how to get help.</li></ul>

PSHE Key Stage 2	• Know how to make informed choices (including recognising that choices can have positive, neutral and negative consequences) and to begin to understand the concept of a 'balanced lifestyle'. • Recognise why and how rules and laws that protect themselves and others are made and enforced, why different rules are needed in different situations and how to take part in making and changing rules. • Understand that everyone has human rights, all peoples and all societies and that children have their own special rights set out in the United Nations Declaration of the Rights of the Child. • Know whom to go to if they are worried and how to attract their attention; ways that pupils can help these people to look after them. • Recognise that they share a responsibility for keeping themselves and others safe, when to say, 'yes', 'no', 'I'll ask' and 'I'll tell'. • Know that these universal rights are there to protect everyone and have primacy both over national law and family and community practices. • Know that there are some cultural practices which are against British law and universal human rights, such as female genital mutilation. • Realise the consequences of anti-social and aggressive behaviours such as bullying and discrimination of individuals and communities. • Know that pressure to behave in an unacceptable, unhealthy or risky way can come from a variety of sources, including people they know and the media. • Know school rules about health and safety, basic emergency aid procedures, where and how to get help. • Know that resources can be allocated in different ways and that these economic choices affect individuals, communities and the sustainability of the environment.

It provides opportunities for children to think about their own values and attitudes and those they encounter in the world around them. What better vehicle for discussion about the rule of law in Britain? And what better opportunity to address the personal safety and safeguarding issues that naturally arise through this subject area? Table 4.1 outlines the links between the rule of law with elements schools address through their PSHE (PSHE Association, 2016).

Introduction

This chapter focuses on defining the rule of law and how it has been understood over time. It will recognise how the historical context has shaped agreement about the rule of law, whilst also considering the application and approaches to laws and rules in schools.

What is the rule of law?

Today, in educational discourse, we hear the expression 'the rule of law', which is a recent phenomenon. The phrase 'rule of law' emerged in September 2014 when it became compulsory for schools to promote British Values (Maylor, 2014). It is clearly set out in Part Two of the Teachers' Standards (Department for Education, 2012b) which states that teachers uphold trust by: 'not undermining fundamental British Values including democracy, the rule of law, individual liberty and mutual respect, and tolerance of those with different faiths and beliefs'. However, whilst an explanation of British Values is given, there is no definition or explanation of each value. Whilst the term 'rule of law' is used in schools, the meaning is not self-evident, which leaves some ambiguity and uncertainty for teachers. At the same time, it offers a certain amount of flexibility for schools to agree their own definition and put their own stamp on what this looks like in practice. Whereas one school may decide it is concerned with a shared code of practice within each classroom, another school may decide the emphasis is upon clear boundaries which are agreed and understood by its pupils. In all schools, rule of law is concerned with everyone who is a member of the school community being accountable and this includes the headteacher, class teachers, parents and pupils.

The definition of 'rule of law' is informed by historical assumptions with ever-changing and contested explanations. The rule of law is fundamentally an important concept and a simple definition may be, 'the prevention of arbitrary governmental action and the protection of individual rights' (Rose, 2004, p.459), although Rose points out that this can appear merely procedural and lacks content. This could make the definition unhelpful and simplistic when it is placed within the school context, but it provides some freedom as schools can ensure that their school beliefs are upheld. In an attempt to strengthen and add content, Kahn (cited in Rose, 2004) suggests that the rule of law is based on our beliefs about who we are, and recognises that 'the people are sovereign, their opinion constitutes all the relevant knowledge, and their representatives possess the only legitimate political power' (p.462). There is a suggestion that the rule of law may lack some logic and that gaining a consensus on the definition may be difficult. However, at the core of our understanding about the rule of law is the knowledge that it is based on having access to a fair and just system where people are not only duty bound, but also profit from laws (Clarke, 2009). The rule of law promotes a civil society which is stable and in which people see laws as a set of rules to be enforced, with order established. Valcke (2012, p.1) explains the rule of law as:

> a concept that describes the supreme authority of the law over governmental action and individual behaviour. It corresponds to a situation where both the government and individuals are bound by the law and comply with it. It is the antithesis of tyrannical or arbitrary rule.

Laws change over time, in response to societal change, but Bellamy (2001) argues that what makes laws valuable is not so much following procedure or rules, but that there has to be some response to ensure those who raise concerns have them answered. The suggestion is that the rule of law meets a particular purpose. For schools this may relate to health and safety or keeping children safe in school – for example, children are asked to walk rather than run around the school; whilst being generic, it is clear to all what behaviour and response is required and it regulates a person's behaviour in a required way. Although the rules of the law are clear, it is also important to note how they are phrased in a positive way, are encouraging and are easy to understand.

Within the understanding of the rule of law, no one is above the law and all must abide by the same laws, which is diametrically opposite to a system that is autocratic. There are many examples of laws that have evolved to protect people and which have been enforced to help create a safer environment, such as wearing a seat belt. In 1983 a law came into force which resulted in drivers and front seat passengers wearing a seatbelt; this was enforced because of the number of deaths from road accidents (Royal Society for the Prevention of Accidents, 2016). Similarly, in 2007, in England, a smoking ban in enclosed places came into force as a direct consequence of the Health Act 2006, after research confirmed the harmful effect to health of cigarette smoke. Such specific laws may result in an interest in the rule of law and this may be seen currently in schools as teachers define what the rule of law means in their settings and how this can develop into a shared understanding between children and adults. There are many good resources on the Parliament website which explain how laws are made and make the topic accessible for teachers and children. Such topic areas may include the study of other cultures and people or, through the History National Curriculum, finding out about the importance of significant figures and events in history. Through the curriculum schools have to provide for the spiritual, moral, social and cultural (SMSC) development of children and, by doing this, they are actively promoting the rule of law. This may be through collective worship as well as providing extra-curricular activities. At the very core of this is the establishment of a strong school ethos and vision which is built upon positive, effective relationships between adults and children. The Department for Education (2014a, p.4) guidelines clearly set out what is required:

It is expected that pupils should understand that while different people may hold different views about what is 'right' and 'wrong', all people living in England are subject to its law. The school's ethos and teaching, which schools should make parents aware of, should support the rule of English civil and criminal law and schools should not teach anything that undermines it. If schools teach about religious law, particular care should be taken to explore the relationship between state and religious law. Pupils should be made aware of the difference between the law of the land and religious law.

Whilst adhering to these guidelines, schools will be able to show how, through their SMSC curriculum, they are meeting the requirements of section 78 of the Education Act 2002. Some of the different activities that schools consider are: through the curriculum area of history, where pupils may look at how the law works in Britain, in contrast to other forms of government in other countries; through geography, where mock panels are held to provide pupils with the opportunity to learn how to argue and defend points of view; or through the use of teaching resources in religious education which can help pupils understand different faiths.

Exploring the development of the rule of law

The rule of law has a long history as an aspect of legal and political systems, but the connection with social equality may have only emerged in the nineteenth century, which is linked to the work of Dicey, 'who perhaps coined the phrase the rule of law' (Rose, 2004, p.457). Dicey (Valcke, 2012) offered three meanings for the rule of law: individual liberty, where the law rules and arbitrary power is excluded, meaning equal subjection to the law; second, and related, is that everyone is equal and no one is above the law; third, there are legal safeguards which protect people and stop any abuse – in pursuit of which the courts are empowered to uphold the rules. It was in 1944 that Hayek (Valcke, 2012) agreed with these ideas and highlighted that the rule of law includes laws that are general and equal, which govern the behaviour of all people. But what does this mean for teachers and how can the rule of law be upheld in schools? One way that schools support the rule of law is to make sure that all pupils have a voice and that this is actively listened to – for example, through classroom discussions in lessons and through sharing their views.

More recently, the rule of law has entered the social and cultural domain with a dedication to develop a democratic and harmonious society. Within the field of education, the rule of law was introduced in 2012 in response to allegations of Muslim extremism (Maylor, 2015). Schools are now required to be active in endorsing British Values, which includes the rule of law as an integral aspect of this. It is also embedded in Part Two of the Teachers' Standards which, as Carroll and Alexander (2016) note, provides a mechanism through which values can be accessed and promoted by teachers.

It remains that recent efforts to define the rule of law have resulted in a confirmation of the different perspectives, reinforcing the multiplicity of understandings. It could be argued that this may offer some flexibility in the way that schools interpret the rule of law, so that personalised laws are defined which support the unique school ethos. Before schools can promote the notion of rule of law, it is clear that the whole school team must agree upon their definition of 'rule of law'.

Laws, rules and the school context

For the rule of law to exist in schools there must be a shared understanding about what this means to the school community. This will be rooted in the school's mission statement and evident in the school ethos. The culture of the school plays a pivotal role in the rule of law, demonstrating a sense of fairness and respect for the law. Practitioners need to establish a vision which will come from their personal and collective values and beliefs. Yet it is not always easy to establish values; we change and reflect over time and external drivers, such as school or government policies, may be influential in this (Taylor and Woolley, 2013). At the very core of this are the children: without them there would be no role for the teacher. A good place to start is:

- to define what the school laws are;

- what these laws are based on;

- what they mean to the children.

There are several key documents that may be drawn upon to inform a school's decisions, which include the Teachers' Standards (Department for Education, 2012b). This clearly outlines British Values and includes eight core principles including fairness, justice, the rule of law and human rights. The Teachers' Standards expect teachers to uphold public trust in the profession, which includes sustaining high ethical standards and behaviour, both within and outside school. Included in this understanding is that teachers must be mindful of upholding British Values.

The School Council

An additional core piece of legislation is the United Nations Convention on the Rights of the Child (United Nations General Assembly, 1991) in which human rights are set out; Taylor and Woolley (2013) highlight that, 'the most significant principle is that children should have the opportunity to express a view on matters of concern to them and to have that view taken seriously' (p.192). There are several schemes that are in place which recognise the child's voice, including whole school activities such as the School Council. This gives elected pupils, from each year group, a chance to meet with other children and staff to discuss issues that are important to them. From the regular meetings, actions are put in place so that children influence change in the school – which may be about any aspect of school life, such as school uniform, school meals or playtimes. This enables each child to have a voice and helps the school to move forward on issues that are important to the children. Another whole school approach is a values-based curriculum where children are able to talk about issues that are important to them, within a safe and supportive climate. The ethos supports everyone in school to reflect upon values and beliefs and how these may be considered in relation to themselves and others within the school and community in which they live. A significant part of creating the school ethos is through collective worship where the expectations are evident through the way that pupils and staff interact with each other and relationships are formed. Alongside whole school activities, classroom-based teaching and learning strategies are used to encourage dialogue in a meaningful way. This may be through children being involved in assessment or the topics they study or through the use of an enquiry-based approach where they raise questions and find the solutions (Cooper, 2014).

It is acknowledged that:

> *It is not necessary for schools or individuals to 'promote' teachings, beliefs or opinions that conflict with their own, but nor is it acceptable for schools to promote discrimination against people or groups on the basis of their belief, opinion or background.*
>
> Department for Education, 2014a, p.6

This suggests that schools must have regard for the rule of law and teachers will draw upon a range of resources from different sources to help pupils understand about different faiths, different perspectives and acceptance that others may hold a different view to them.

Each of these possibilities enables choices to be made about how the children and adults behave within the setting. This is apparent in how they interact with each other, through the curriculum, in actions and words, in what is said, how it is said and in how everyone behaves. This is the foundation for making rules about the way everyone in the school would like to live whilst having regard for promoting British Values.

The rule of law in the school and classroom

Rules and systems

Rules are evident in society, for without them there would be disorder and chaos. A school operates as a society, with its own specific rules used to keep everyone in school safe and to enable an efficient orderly place to exist. Rules set out the expected standards for behaviour and attitudes, although, as Petty (2004) points out, 'There is a difference between authoritarianism and the vigorous use of legitimate authority' (p.122). It is important to remember that teachers are there to support learning and to support the academic and social development of each child; they are not police officers. Law enforcement is not an add-on, but part of the atmosphere and environment, rooted in values and beliefs. The school is a community and rules should be for the benefit of everyone, applied fairly and consistently. Through acceptance and ownership of the rules there is more likelihood that they will be respected and valued. This impacts upon how each person will demonstrate that they are playing a responsible part as a member of the school community, including upholding the school's values and processes. Through following rules within a school setting, the foundations are being laid for children, as they grow and develop towards adulthood, to follow the law within a wider, civilised society. This includes supporting children to make the right choices, which in turn helps them to feel empowered. A variety of different strategies are employed by schools to ensure a fair system is implemented. These are discussed next.

Home–school contract

Many schools use a contract setting out the school's expectations and the responsibilities of school staff, parents and children which are lawful and reasonable. The contract is sent to all parents and, on signing it, they agree to the school's aims and values, which detail how the school is responsible for its pupils and what the pupils' and parents' responsibilities are. The governing body of the school is also involved in making sure the parents understand their role in their child's education within the school. Every school is unique, so the contract will need to set out very clearly the ethos of the school. This can be defined through the relationships between staff, between children and between staff and children, and is integral to the school's aims and vision. The home–school contract may include expectations for attendance and punctuality, discipline and behaviour, homework, how and what information is shared between parents and school. Through parents and school working together the contract can support the aim for children to become responsible and empowered. The aim is clear, to work in partnership to ensure all are successful, so that teachers and pupils can work in a positive learning climate.

Behaviour and attendance policy

All schools are required to have an up-to-date policy setting out the school's expectations for behaviour and attendance (Department for Education, 2012a). The aim is to provide a framework for behaviour and the promotion of a positive learning environment in which all staff and pupils feel safe. This is used to inform pupils, parents and all school staff about the school's guidelines and expectations for behaviour. The policy should be implemented in a way that shows fairness, equality and respect to every pupil. Schools will utilise different strategies to ensure the policy is effective and is being used consistently. The following examples are some of the ways schools manage this, but are not intended as a prescriptive list:

- teachers and pupils discuss and agree school and class rules;

- pupils with emotional and behavioural needs are supported with additional resources;

- a clear framework for rewards and sanctions is applied;

- there is whole school professional development on behaviour for learning;

- poor attendance is followed up with parents;

- a whole school reward system is in place to reward pupils with full attendance over a term;

- via the curriculum, teaching and learning resources are used to promote positive behaviour through engagement with learning;

- a system is used to follow up on any absence which has not been explained.

Consider other systems, whole school- and classroom-based, which you have seen in school, that are used to support an effective behaviour and attendance policy.

Schools, parents and pupils have a responsibility for behaviour and attendance. Every school has a legal duty to ensure pupils attend school through being pro-active in the way it encourages pupils to attend. There is also a requirement to inform parents of the school's absence figures. In the same way, parents have a duty and that is to make sure that their child attends school and is ready for learning. The role of a headteacher and class teacher is to show a commitment to working with parents and pupils, to make sure that behaviour and attendance are of a high standard.

In conclusion, Valcke (2012) provides a reminder that even government leaders and eminent citizens have struggled to express exactly what is meant by rule of law. Maylor (2014) adds that many teachers also struggle to articulate their understanding of a shared vision. Within schools the debate continues to reach a consensus about whether the rule of law encompasses the rights of individual members of the community, or a more formal contract which is applied to all to ensure there is no abuse, or whether equality and democracy is a defining feature. The different viewpoints and contested definitions suggest that schools will adapt their understanding to meet their needs and that this can be viewed as 'analogous to the notion of the good, in the sense that everyone is for it, but have contrasting convictions about what it is' (Maylor, 2014, p.1). Although schools will vary and have different views about how law and order is interpreted, it needs to be made clear that it is for the benefit of the whole school community, and both pupils and adults need to have a shared understanding of the rules.

The importance of the delivery of the rule of law in Britain as part of the British Values requirements

As outlined above, this particular British Value has an uncertain history, but is, nevertheless, one of the most concrete of the values set by government, and one which impacts in a very real way on every single person's life. It is undoubtedly for this reason that it is one which seems to have immediate 'kerb appeal' in the classroom. It links beautifully with the experiences of every child as being part of the school system and many will be able to make links between this learning and their 'real-life' experiences. It is also, however, a subject that, arguably, well deserves to be a compulsory one, pivotal as it is to pupils' understanding and appreciation of citizenship and their place as a citizen in society.

CASE STUDY: EXPLORING THE RULE OF LAW WITH CHILDREN

Jenny is a teacher in her second year of teaching. She undertook the teaching of a series of studies of the rule of law in Britain with her Year 5 and 6 class as part of their British Values learning connected to the PSHE curriculum. Although this was her first formal foray into British Values with the class, the children were well versed in and comfortable with the concept and application of values since the school prioritises this as part of its ethos and curriculum. Their baseline understanding of the rule of law in their country was, however, limited. Initial questioning revealed a rudimentary understanding: 'Laws help us grow up; they keep us safe; you get punished if you do something wrong.'

Learning took the form of an exposition, through a Powerpoint presentation about where laws are made, who makes them and why, through to the differences between criminal and civil law. From the outset, the children responded enthusiastically to the subject matter and became quickly immersed in the exchange of views, speculation and wonder about our judicial system. It was easy to see that, because all the children had, in fact, some knowledge of a law that affected them directly (such as the law about wearing a seat belt in a car or the age at which it is

(Continued)

permissible to drive a tractor), they were deeply engaged in a meaningful learning experience, pooling their knowledge and generating a decidedly positive attitude to finding out more.

KEY QUESTIONS

- Where would you have started with your teaching approach to this British Value?
- What pedagogies can a school employ to ensure that this learning is 'real' and relevant to children?
- What can the school do to ensure all children are able to access what could be an abstract concept?

It could be said that Jenny was lucky: her class were quickly engaged and motivated by this topic and the lesson had a propulsion and momentum, which rendered it a very successful experience. Other classes may have shown more diffidence or even lack of engagement. One way in to this topic may have been to set some pre-learning tasks, to carry out a questionnaire with their families at home, or a challenge such as list as many laws you know in ten minutes. Another (almost) foolproof strategy is to introduce the subject using a film clip. There are no rights and wrongs, of course, but teachers do undoubtedly need a degree of familiarity and certainly a rapport with the class for a successful discussion or debate to happen. This scenario looked at a one-off lesson, delivered by the class teacher, but clearly laid bare the potential for future discussions, debates and activities: how vast is the potential for tapping into children's curiosity here!

Strategies for teaching about the rule of law in Britain

For any school-based strategy to be successful it is important for education professionals to understand how children learn. Critically, enabling children to focus on the British Value of the rule of law is to give them agency – that is, put them in control of their thinking, outlook and actions by enabling them to understand why we have laws, what they are and what they do, and what effect they have on our (and other) societies. Chaille and Halverson, in their article 'Issues in education: teaching ethics: the role of the classroom teacher' (2004), remind us that review of research into character education going back to the 1920s found that didactic methods alone – such as teacher exhortation and stories read but not discussed with the pupils – were ineffective in promoting moral conduct. So too was the teaching of simple reasoning and thinking strategies alone, or learning experiences that had no relation to a child's own social experience. This leads us to the conclusion that learning in this context, as much as any other, must appeal to children, must resonate with them on a personal level and fundamentally touch them. Deci and Ryan (2000) draw attention to the need for learning to be fun in order to effectively address one of children's basic psychological needs, namely the need for fun, adventure and enjoyable experiences, and feeds into other basic needs, such as competence, autonomy and relatedness.

CASE STUDY: CHILDREN'S NEGATIVE EXPERIENCES

Be alert to safeguarding issues arising with this work.

Not all children's experiences of the rule of law in this country will be positive. There will be children who have or have had a parent arrested and/or in prison, as well as those whose family households hold the law in low esteem. Some will have had direct experience of social services and will have been taught mistrust of those who hold legal authority. For some, it may be as for Jake in Year 6, whose personal experience of police raids at his house, the threat of being taken in to care and his witnessing of violence in the family home and its consequences sharpened his appetite to find out more about this subject. In tackling this area, the teacher, fully aware and mindful of events, was careful to contextualise this learning in a positive way, emphasising how laws are there to keep us safe, how the United Nations Charter of the Rights of the Child specifically speaks to children all over the world, and how every law subject to scrutiny can be found to have the value of care at its core.

KEY QUESTIONS

- How can these strategies be built into a progressive and developmental experience for children across the school?
- How might parents be involved in supporting the school's teaching and approach?

Some schools have found it helpful to outline their approach to teaching and learning of British Values to parents through school newsletters, leaflets or the school website. Others are very aware of the need to inspire positive approaches to community policing and law-keeping and, to this end, adopt a concerted programme of welcoming professionals into school and provide opportunities for pupils and their families to engage with them, such as through talking to children in assemblies, inviting them to come to the school fête and to attend school plays and events. All this helps to integrate, as one headteacher put it, 'the outside in'. She went on to describe how families in their community had traditionally been wary of police and local community officers, and how this distrust often extended to medical and school professionals too, but how, bit by bit, she could see positive relationships building because of her school's proactive and determined bid to break down the barriers.

CASE STUDY: INCLUDING ALL CHILDREN

Be alert to safeguarding issues arising with this work.

For Benjamina, a looked-after child in Year 5, this subject area was also to have deep and often painful resonance. Knowing her background and some of the issues Benjamina had already had to face in her young life, her teacher was able to skilfully craft the material he used with this in mind. In line with a discussed and agreed school policy on the teaching of British Values, she was, however, careful not to have a 'no admittance' approach too, so that when negative comments were made or alluded to they could be sensitively and respectfully handled. That way, Benjamina was subtly helped to feel that this was a subject area about which she had as much right as anyone to engage with. In carefully approaching the learning in this way, the teacher found that, for Benjamina, it sharpened her appetite to engage. No one could claim that it brought about a whole-hearted conversion in her private attitudes and allegiances to a family culture, but it most certainly added to her breadth and depth of understanding of how this fitted into a wider picture of society. Importantly, this teacher did not observe anything that made her uneasy in terms of the Prevent agenda, but she was mindful that this is a possibility and knew the procedures set out by her school in the event of any concern.

KEY QUESTIONS

- What can a school do to promote the inclusion of pupils with concerns?
- How can the school ensure safeguarding points are built into teaching and learning?
- Do staff know what to do if they have any concerns about radicalisation of a child in their care?

Clearly, our work in schools on British Values sits centrally in a carefully considered whole school approach to inclusion, safeguarding, special educational needs and equality, and to the teaching of PSHE and citizenship. All staff must be fully aware, as Benjamina's teacher was, of the school's policies and approach, and must emulate and adhere to these. All staff, teaching and non-teaching, should have recent and up-to-date knowledge of procedures and processes in relation to the Prevent agenda, in particular, and be mindful of their duty to report any concerns. Many, if not most, teachers in primary schools have a pretty good working knowledge about the backgrounds and circumstances of the children in their care; work hard to establish, build and maintain great working relationships with parents and carers; and are diligent about attending safeguarding, Common Assessment Framework (CAF) meetings and special educational needs reviews. In other words, they care deeply about the individual and want to craft their teaching to support individual as well as whole class learning. Teaching and learning about British Values highlights the need for this kind of approach to teaching like almost nothing else.

Values into action!

Here are some suggested strategies that may be part of this whole school approach and/or work as a 'getting started' one-off session:

- starting – or baseline – discussion: why do we have laws?

- relate to school rules: why do we have them, what would life be like without them?

- relate to religious education learning about God's Ten Commandments to Moses: what are the links here? Research rules of other religions;

- quick challenge: how many laws can you think of that you already know?

- share a Powerpoint or similar about British laws, outlining what they are, why we have them, who makes them and how; show footage of the Houses of Parliament and law courts;

- challenge the class to make a pamphlet for parents about the rule of law in Britain;

- design and then justify your new law. What is it designed to do? Who is it aimed at? How will it change your community/the country if it is implemented? Have a class vote to determine the most popular idea;

- make a class or personal presentation for assembly, or for a public speaking event. Invite parents and record it so that their involvement is maximised;

- follow up by writing to your local MP with your new law idea: he/she may even write back!

- invite your local MP to come and talk about law-making;

- research the wackiest law that ever existed – for example, the one that banned the eating of mince pies on Christmas day;

- rank reasons for laws in order of importance;

- research laws in other countries: how do they differ from our own and why might this be?

- start to map them into the curriculum: create a specific place in planning formats to ensure that links are made;

- ensure specific attention is paid to safeguarding opportunities, such as knowing that these universal rights are there to protect everyone and have primacy both over national law and family and community practices, knowing that there are some cultural practices which are against British law and universal human rights, such as female genital mutilation and realising the consequences of anti-social and aggressive behaviours such as bullying and discrimination of individuals and communities;

- carry out an audit: how and where can this British Value link into other areas of the curriculum?

- involve pupils in creating a school display to exemplify this British Value;

- arrange to visit the House of Commons – see where it all happens!

A SUMMARY OF KEY POINTS FROM THIS CHAPTER

- Schools have a statutory duty to teach pupils about British Values in a way that is commensurate with the age and ability of its pupils, regardless of its context.
- The rule of law is a key British Value, linked to citizenship and PSHE, as well as the Prevent agenda.
- Pedagogy is all-important in teaching about the rule of law for British Values: it must be meaningful, relevant and fun.

- The teaching of all British Values, including the rule of law, must support pupils with learning difficulties and wellbeing needs.
- Effective teaching involves working with parents.
- The school needs to support pupils using a developmental and progressive curriculum approach.
- Schools may wish to seek outside support from other agencies to promote this teaching and learning.
- Schools must be mindful of safeguarding issues in relation to teaching about this area of British Values, and must be cognisant of their duties to report any suspected radicalisation.

References

Bellamy, R. (2001) 'The rule of law and the rule of persons'. *Critical Review of International Social and Political Philosophy,* 4 (4): 221–51.

Campbell, J.M. (2010) 'Importance of rule of law to civil society'. *Defense Counsel Journal,* 77 (3), 287–8.

Carroll, J. and Alexander, G. (2016) *The Teachers' Standards in Primary Schools: Understanding and Evidencing Effective Practice.* London: SAGE.

Chaille, C. and Halverson, S. (2004) 'Issues in education: teaching ethics: the role of the classroom teacher'. *Childhood Education,* 80 (3): 157–8, DOI: 10.1080/00094056.2004.10522795

Clarke, A. (2009) 'Civil justice: the importance of the rule of law'. *International Lawyer,* 43 (1): 39–44.

Cooper, H. (2014) *Professional Studies in Primary Education.* London: SAGE.

Deci, E.L. and Ryan, R.M. (2000) 'The "what" and "why" of goal pursuits: human needs and the self-determination of behaviour'. *Psychological Inquiry,* 11: 227–68.

Department for Education (2012a) Behaviour and Discipline in schools. Guidance for Governing Bodies. London: Department for Education.

Department for Education (2012b) Teachers' Standards. DFE-00066-2011. London: Department for Education.

Department for Education (2014a) *Promoting Fundamental British Values as Part of SMSC in Schools: Departmental Advice for Maintained Schools.* London: Department for Education.

Maylor, U. (2014) 'Promoting British Values opens up a can of worms for teachers'. *Guardian*.

Parliament UK (n.d.) Available at: http://www.parliament.uk/education/teaching-resources-lesson-plans?cat=lawmaking (accessed 12 December 2017).

Petty, G. (2014) *Teaching Today*. 4th edn. Cheltenham: Nelson Thornes.

PSHE Association (2016) www.pshe-association.org.uk (accessed 12 December 2017).

Rose, J. (2004) 'The rule of law in the western world: an overview'. *Journal of Social Philosophy*, 35: 457–70.

Royal Society for the Prevention of Accidents (n.d.) Available at: http://www.rospa.com/campaigns-fundraising/success/seatbelts/ (accessed 24 August 2016).

Smoke Free England (n.d.) Available at: http://www.smokefreeengland.co.uk/what-do-i-do/quick-guide/ (accessed 24 August 2016).

Taylor, K. and Woolley, R. (2013) *Values and Vision in Primary Education*. Maidenhead: Open University Press.

United Nations General Assembly (1991) United Nations Convention on the Rights of the Child.

Valcke, A. (2012) The rule of law: its origins and meanings (a short guide for practitioners) Social Science Research Network Paper. Available at: http://ssrn.com/abstract=2042336 (accessed 25 August 2016).

Further reading

Department for Education (2014b) National Curriculum for England Framework Document. London: DfE.

Duckworth, J. (2009) *The Little Book of Values: Educating Children to Become Thinking, Responsible and Caring Citizens*. Carmarthen: Crown House.

Farrer, F. (2000) *A Quiet Revolution*. London: Rider.

Hawkes, N. (2002) *How to Inspire and Develop Positive Values in Your Classroom*. Cambridge: LDA.

Hawkes, N. (2015) *From My Heart: Transforming Lives Through Values*. Carmarthen: Crown House.

OFSTED (2016) *Handbook for Schools in England*. London: OFSTED.

5
MUTUAL RESPECT AND TOLERANCE

This chapter explores:

- the importance of mutual respect and tolerance in Britain as part of the British Values requirements and in relation to the Prevent programme;
- the importance of a whole school approach to teaching about mutual respect and individual tolerance in the primary school;
- how these British Values fit into statutory requirements;
- strategies that promote the effective delivery of the concept of mutual respect and tolerance in Britain as part of the British Values requirements;
- the importance of these values in promoting a whole school, inclusive environment.

Teachers' Standards

This chapter supports the development of the following Teachers' Standards:

TS1: Set high expectations which inspire, motivate and challenge pupils:

- a safe and stimulating environment for pupils, rooted in mutual respect;
- set goals that stretch and challenge pupils of all backgrounds, abilities and dispositions.

TS7: Manage behaviour effectively to ensure a good and safe learning environment:

- manage classes effectively, using approaches which are appropriate to pupils' needs in order to involve and motivate them.

Within the Teachers' Standards, TS1 has a focus upon ethos and environment. Integral to this is a requirement to follow the school's policies and to promote expected behaviours which are rooted in mutual respect. This is achieved through building strong, positive relationships with pupils. As a role model, a teacher must also exhibit the behaviours expected through being aware of interactions between teachers and pupils, between pupil and pupil and between adults. TS3 subject knowledge, and TS4 planning offer opportunities for a teacher to demonstrate an appreciation of other cultures and faiths. Additionally, teachers have flexibility in their planning to include engaging activities which can support pupils to share their views as well as understand the views of others within a safe, trusting classroom environment. Relationships are a central focus of TS7, which highlights how teachers manage behaviour to ensure a positive learning environment is maintained. Teachers act with authority to respond to unacceptable behaviours, as well as acting decisively in line with the school behaviour policy. This includes promoting courteous behaviour between children and between children and adults. TS8 is concerned with the wider professional responsibilities of a teacher. These include how teachers communicate with parents about their child's wellbeing, which recognises the pastoral responsibility of a teacher. In their role, teachers have a responsibility to promote common shared values between parents and teachers. Mutual respect and tolerance, it is argued (Maylor, 2016), have developed over time and contribute to the shared values held and jointly owned across the UK.

Whilst a child is in a teacher's care, the teacher takes on an *in loco parentis* role to behave and respond as any responsible parent would. The further personal and professional responsibilities of a teacher are set out in Part Two of the Teachers' Standards and running throughout is the link to values and beliefs to ensure that public trust in the teaching profession is upheld. This takes into account the duty a teacher has to follow school policies and practices, as well as statutory frameworks, not only whilst carrying out their professional duties, but also in their expression of personal beliefs. The impact of the standards is rooted in the context of performance, with a clear connection between the Teachers' Standards and appraisal. Elton-Chalcraft et al. (2017) suggest that effective practice for teachers should include professional development that encompasses how British Values are understood. This includes attending external training opportunities, personal research and reading, and online courses, as well as the professional discussions that are presented in schools.

Part Two: Personal and professional conduct

Teachers uphold public trust in the profession and maintain high standards of ethics and behaviour, within and outside school, by:

- treating pupils with dignity, building relationships rooted in mutual respect, and at all times observing proper boundaries appropriate to a teacher's professional position;

- not undermining fundamental British Values, including democracy, the rule of law, individual liberty and mutual respect, and tolerance of those with different faiths and beliefs;

- ensuring that personal beliefs are not expressed in ways which exploit pupils' vulnerability or might lead them to break the law.

Introduction

This chapter will focus on defining mutual respect and tolerance, as well as examining the role they now play in aspects of our daily lives in schools. The EU Referendum Result Department for Education Update states the importance of this:

> *All schools will continue to play an important role in promoting the fundamental British values of mutual respect and tolerance for those of all backgrounds and faiths. We are clear that no child should live in fear of racism or bullying, and by law all schools must have a behaviour policy with measures to tackle bullying.*

Department for Education, 2016, p.1

Furthermore, this chapter will seek to examine such values and how such concepts are understood by pupils, as well as how these values relate to statutory requirements and may be promoted under the Teachers' Standards (Department for Education, 2012). It will also examine strategies for the successful integration of mutual respect and tolerance within the whole school's curriculum, management and organisation.

Respect and tolerance of those with different faiths and beliefs

The wording of the Teachers' Standards (TS) (Department for Education, 2012) clearly places an emphasis on morals and principles, and aligns with a pedagogy of values in education. Identified within this is a respect for the tolerance of other cultures alongside valuing the rights of others to ensure that British Values are not undermined. Yet, defining values within the context of Britishness remains a challenge and some would argue that particular values may not be unique to being British. Values exist within a social context and schools have to maintain the balance of supporting individuals to share agreed British Values whilst recognising that we live in a multicultural society.

Maintenance and prevention

The responsibility of teachers not to undermine British Values supports the government's expectations. This includes two central themes, those of maintenance and prevention. From a maintenance perspective, teachers uphold the vision of promoting community cohesion whilst being mindful of addressing potential negative thoughts from children, which may be concerned with radicalisation. Upholding an ideology is promoted through the Teachers' Standards and it is argued that schools are best placed to support this, as centres of learning, both on an academic and social level.

As a multinational society, mutual respect and tolerance have influenced British culture over many years. Within a multicultural society Britain enjoys a diverse range of identities and cultures, making the agreement of a set of common, shared principles important. These values have been developed over time and space, are rooted in fairness and aim to ensure that people can live in a tolerant society. A diverse society recognises the significance of a range of diverse values which encompasses minority ethnic communities (Maylor, 2016). There are also the challenges of maintaining and upholding shared values and living in a diverse culture, as highlighted by Biale et al. (2017). In providing a context to widen a society's perspectives, there is the potential to disturb social cohesion and for conflict among groups to emerge. Viewing this from an educational perspective is justified as the philosophy is central to developing a cohesive, unified community, whilst understanding that there are different ways to construct identities. The understanding at a macro-level is mirrored at the local level within a school community in the way that parents, children, teachers and governors work together.

Yet, the approach from the government's standpoint may be viewed as a shift towards prevention as it centres upon promoting British Values. The notion of prevention brings out the importance of working with communities to address the deeper causes seen to lead individuals to extremism. Significant changes to the Equality law in 2010 (Bhopal and Rhamie, 2014) highlighted to schools that they cannot discriminate against pupils because of their religion or beliefs. Whilst there is no question that schools place priority upon and support this view, they are now additionally accountable for the political agendas relating to anti-terrorism (Elton-Chalcraft et al., 2017). Recognised within this position, Maylor (2016) suggests there are three key themes for teachers to address:

- to respect and tolerate people of different faiths and beliefs;
- to develop confidence in challenging pupil racism;
- to deal assertively with inappropriate comments.

This provides a starting point for understanding the area of mutual respect and tolerance alongside placing this in the context of faith and beliefs. Included here are the factors of relationships, behaviour and attitudes, those of both teachers and children, which are aspects of good practice and are addressed within this chapter.

Thoughts about mutual respect and tolerance must be evident in a school's planning, so now we will consider how you might approach this.

The relationship between the National Curriculum and British Values: mutual respect and tolerance

The value of mutual respect and tolerance can be located both explicitly and implicitly in the National Curriculum for primary schools. It is worth knowing the places where it arises, so that direct links can be made.

What is mutual respect and tolerance?

The notion of mutual respect and tolerance linked to British Values is possibly one of the most important and obvious values to teach to adults, young people and children. Given the mobility of the world's population, allied with many recent cultural and diversity issues relating to issues such as race, religious, faith and culture in society, this value has become increasingly complex and diverse for children to appreciate and understand. This, combined with the significant role it plays in promoting an inclusive society, makes it a fundamentally important value to promote.

Table 5.1 *Links to the National Curriculum: mutual respect and tolerance*

PSHE Key Stage 1	• Know about Children's Rights and Human Rights. • Share opinions on things that matter to them and explain their views through discussions. • Listen to other people and play and work cooperatively (including strategies to resolve simple arguments through negotiation). Recognise what is fair and unfair, kind and unkind, what is right and wrong. • Recognise when people are being unkind either to them or others.
PSHE Key Stage 2	• Research, discuss and debate topical issues, problems and events concerning health and wellbeing and offer their recommendations to appropriate people. • Recognise that they may experience conflicting emotions and when they might need to listen to their emotions or overcome them. • Understand that everyone has human rights, all peoples and all societies, and that children have their own special rights set out in the United Nations Declaration of the Rights of the Child. • Recognise that they share a responsibility for keeping themselves and others safe, when to say, 'yes', 'no', 'I'll ask' and 'I'll tell'. • Know that these universal rights are there to protect everyone and have primacy both over national law and family and community practices. • Realise the consequences of anti-social and aggressive behaviours such as bullying and discrimination of individuals and communities. • Resolve differences by looking at alternatives, seeing and respecting others' points of view, making decisions and explaining choices. • Appreciate the range of national, regional, religious and ethnic identities in the United Kingdom.
Science	• Tolerance in relation to living things and their interdependence.
History	• To know how people's lives have shaped this nation and how Britain has influenced and been influenced by the wider world.
Geography	• To understand the processes that give rise to key physical and human geographical features of the world, how these are interdependent and how they bring about spatial variation and change over time.
Languages	• The ability to converse in another language (and to think in another language), leading to the ability to connect with others beyond our cultural and geographical borders.
Design and technology	• The role of tolerance and understanding in relation to the process of critiquing and testing products and ideas.
Art	• The role of tolerance in the appreciation of different forms of art.
Music	• Tolerance, leading to appreciation of music across a range of historical periods, genres, styles and traditions, including the works of the great composers and musicians.

Each school, owing to its individual demographics, may find context-specific issues that centre on the need to display tolerance and to show mutual respect for others. Though such a value may seem especially vital to promote in inner-city locations, you must remember that culturally diverse communities inhabit all areas of the UK. For example, with the growth of the number of seasonal workers for picking crops in the Home Counties and the Welsh Marches, together with many other areas of the UK, schools in these areas may experience influxes of pupils from many countries and cultures during such periods of time. Similarly, some schools may have pupils attend their school on occasion from more nomadic lifestyles such as Gypsy, Roma and Travellers (GR&T). Such variance in school communities can itself promote opportunities for ignorance and intolerance to flourish among pupils who do not fully understand such lifestyles and people and therefore do not see the reason to be inclusive towards them.

It could be suggested that given such a backdrop there is now, more than ever, a vital need to encourage children to be tolerant and to show mutual respect for others to promote a harmonious future and society. Furthermore, it is also vital that we teach pupils to appreciate the similarities and to celebrate the differences so that others are accepted and valued (Woolley, 2013). This is important if we are to achieve such a vital inclusive goal linked to this significant value. Given these cultural and diverse changes to society it would seem more important than ever that the educators of our children and the schools that they attend should promote what should be seen as: 'quality education to prevent violence, to strengthen a climate of tolerance and security, and to foster the development of values of peace, tolerance, and mutual understanding as well as capacities for the non-violent resolution of conflicts' (Pigozzi, 2006, p.3).

Not only should the promotion of this value be seen as fundamentally and morally important, but you should also realise the statutory importance and nature of your work around this topic. Schools have a statutory obligation under the Race Relations (Amendment) Act 2000 to comply with local authority procedures for recording, reporting and responding to racist incidents. In addition to this the Equality Act 2010 (Department for Education, 2014b) has significance for schools and teachers when it comes to supporting the mutual respect and tolerance for others. For example, this Act states that the curriculum should not be delivered in a discriminatory way and that all forms of prejudice-motivated bullying are dealt with equally, firmly and seriously in schools. This Act (Department for Education, 2014b, p.8) also makes it clear that it is 'unlawful for a school to discriminate against a pupil or prospective pupil by treating them less favourably' because of aspects such as, race and religion or belief. Government guidance (Department for Education, 2014b) clearly suggests that it is by educating individuals that they may be equipped not only to challenge prejudice but, importantly, also to be responsible for their own actions. Through the school's use of SMSC (Department for Education, 2014a) children are encouraged to learn how to promote cultural respect and also show tolerance and harmony towards other faiths and traditions. Unfortunately, such an aspiration is not without some degree of difficulty. For many children the current influence of the media and the range of opinions encountered in their home lives mean that the impact of stereotyping, prejudice and bigotry is all too prevalent in their developing and often preconceived view of the world. Such a situation therefore makes the role of education with regard to this value more difficult than ever. Thus, the importance of such work is not only that of a moral imperative, but also a right for our children. As the UN Convention on the Rights of the Child (UNCRC) (UNESCO, 1989, p.11) suggests under Article 29, we should prepare a child for a 'responsible life in a free society, in the spirit of understanding, peace, tolerance, equality of sexes, and friendship among all peoples, ethnic, national and religious groups and persons of indigenous origin'.

All such themes are closely allied to the way that children freely live their everyday lives without fear of bullying, intimidation or being unable to speak out to challenge such prejudices. As such, much of a school's work with regard to advancing such ideas will not only be linked to schools' and teachers' practice, but will also be embedded in school policy. These may include policies linked to whole school behaviour, anti-bullying, e-safety, equality and diversity. It is important to note that, with regard to behaviour policies, as Bhopal and Myers (2009, p.310) comment, good practice indicates that they should: 'recognise ... division in communities at large and reflect ... a concern to provide a moral context for the response to, and management of any inherent issues'.

Integral to any policy requirements is the ability for you as a teacher to follow such school policies and by doing so be able to promote the expected behaviours which are rooted in mutual respect and tolerance. Such personal and professional responsibilities are clearly set out in Part Two of the Teachers' Standards. Running throughout Part Two is the link to values and beliefs to ensure public trust in the teaching profession is upheld. This takes into account the duty that you as a teacher have to follow school policies and practices, as well as statutory frameworks, whilst carrying out not only professional duties, but also in the expression of your personal beliefs. The impact of the standards is rooted in the context of performance, with a clear connection between the Teachers' Standards and appraisal. There is an agreement that effective practice to support teachers to understand what is meant by British Values includes access to professional development (Elton-Chalcraft et al., 2017). This includes attending external training opportunities, personal research and reading, and online courses, as well as the professional discussions that are presented in schools.

Relationships are key to promoting an ethos of mutual respect and tolerance. Schools should be conscious of the negative impact that pupils' actions may have on one another – such as name calling. These actions must be recognised by the whole school community as being unacceptable whatever the reason or pupil's justification behind them. Schools should act swiftly to deal with and eradicate such breaches of pupil tolerance between one another if this value is to be upheld.

The key to supporting mutual respect and tolerance successfully in schools and your individual classroom should be seen by you as involving the need to build strong, positive relationships with pupils in your care. As a role model, it is imperative that you also exhibit the behaviours expected in order to promote this value positively, that you are aware of the value of being a positive role model not only in terms of interactions between you and your pupils, but also when dealing with adults in your setting. Such positive modelling of good practice is vital if you wish children to emulate the expectations you have for creating individuals who truly value mutual respect and tolerance.

Though Maylor (2016) identifies many important issues when considering the teaching of tolerance and of mutual respect, it is important that you do not, unlike teachers and schools outlined in this study, blame the lack of student diversity or parental/pupil ignorance of the range of ethnic groups for you or your setting failing to challenge racism. It is important that you remain sensitive to the complexities of individual British identities so that you as a teacher can not only build a more comprehensive view of the range of backgrounds in your class, but that you may also avoid assuming that pupils might be 'immigrants rather than British born' (Maylor, 2016, p.325).

Teaching and learning: mutual respect and tolerance

The curriculum can provide a rich means to plan for and to explore the notion of mutual respect and tolerance as part of teaching and learning. Although this value is both implicit and explicit within the primary curriculum, it is also prevalent in and critical to the learning process itself. Learning to get along with other people, playing and working with people who are very different from ourselves is one of the first challenges of school! Throughout life it emerges as a continued test of a character. Added to this are the challenges posed by different ways of working (independently, in a group) in a host of different contexts and settings. We learn that we need other people to help us, that our feelings towards them and views about them can change in the light of our own needs, and, what's more, that we can grow to like people the more we get to know them. Given this, it is important that the school and that you map opportunities to promote the teaching of this value in the curriculum so that vital learning opportunities are not missed. Perhaps it may be a good idea to create a specific place in your current planning formats to ensure that such positive links are made to this value. A possible starting point for understanding and planning of the area of mutual respect and tolerance is that of placing this value into the context of faith, cultures and beliefs. As a successful teacher, you will know the children well and be able to plan with a consideration of their needs. Although there are many elements of planning, including having clear learning objectives, assessment and ensuring pupil progress, the focus here is upon the link between planning and supporting children to develop a respectful and tolerant attitude towards others. This includes guiding children to share their own views whilst developing the idea that although it is acceptable to have a view that is different from others, they must learn respect for others with different views. As Carroll and Alexander (2016) highlight in relation to planning, the focus needs to be upon the outcome and learning, rather than the task.

With regard to TS3 relating to subject knowledge and TS4, planning and teaching, there are opportunities for you as a teacher to demonstrate accountability for values as well as their understanding of other cultures and faiths. Additionally, you will have the flexibility in your planning to include engaging activities which can support pupils to share their views as well as understand the views of others within a safe, trusting classroom environment.

A few examples of how you can link this value to the curriculum include the following:

- art and design can help an individual to understand the need for tolerance of other people's ideas whilst promoting an understanding of different cultures and artistic styles such as the role that artistic expression plays in Islamic art;

- music and dance allows pupils to reflect on their own and others' cultural identity, as well as promoting mutual respect for a range of artistic expression. For example, Bhangra, offers an expressive form of dance in the UK but originated in the Punjab region of India;

- religious education can lead to an understanding of mutual respect and tolerance through the study of customs, festivals and religious characteristics. Festivals that you might see considered in primary schools are Baisakhi, Diwali and Holi;

- history, as well as drama, can promote understanding and empathy for different moral and ethical issues around race, faith and cultures – for example, the Second World War and the Holocaust;

- geography can allow children to develop a sense of place. It can also help them to consider the complex issues around community and other people's society. Unfortunately, given the current issues around migrants, this too may form a means to help develop compassion, tolerance and understanding of others and their fate.

Additionally, when you are planning it will be important to allow time to explore an area of a value such as mutual respect and tolerance which could include the following teaching strategies:

- class debates. Consider the idea of the role of charities and events such as Red Nose day and present views on how they stereotype less-economically developed countries as 'poor'. What does the word 'poor' mean? Is this just about material possessions?

- individual children taking on the role of another to present a point of view. The use of photographs offers a great opportunity for children to take on the role of a person in the picture and discuss how they feel, what they can see, hear, taste or smell. Not only can this be used to challenge stereotyping, but it can also address children's misconceptions;

- groups of children representing a specific group such as residents of an area can support children to understand other points of view;

- research in classroom projects on topical issues in the news or when teaching about a distant locality, or finding out about other faiths;

- raising ideas for children to consider whether they are fact or fiction can lead to some interesting discussion;

- communication through a partnership school, either in a distant locality or within the UK. This experience can support children when looking at the ways their lives are the same as, as well as different from, children in other places, and to appreciate diversity.

As you engage children in such reflective activities you will be supporting and developing a trusting classroom ethos when discussing this value as part of your curriculum. You should also explore your own values to ensure that you hold no prejudice or stereotype regarding any specific groups of people. This is challenging but all part of the process when seeking opportunities to promote trust and respect in the classroom.

As well as mutual respect and tolerance being driven by aspects of the curriculum, this value can be linked to the school's personal, health, social and citizenship education (PHSCE). Through opportunities such as circle time, aspects of social emotional aspects of learning (SEAL), visiting speakers from culturally different groups and faiths can play a role in discussing and understanding this value.

Opportunities to consider the tolerance for others and the need for mutual respect may be sought through daily assemblies when considering famous people's lives, such as those of Gandhi or Martin Luther King Jnr. Stories linked to the many world faiths can also allow pupils to develop an understanding of this value. Involving children in activities such as 'faith days' to celebrate festivals from other religions provides for an understanding of the need for diversity in our society. Other activities that allow for an understanding and development of this value could include the following:

- eating differing food types and considering how different food may need to be prepared by different religious groups;

- trips to different places of worship, such as a gurdwara;

- dressing up in clothes from different cultures (care and consideration must be given to avoid any possible preconceived ideas and stereotypes);

- using world news, such as the ongoing crisis of refugees, to think about the significance of mutual respect and tolerence;

- through the use of story, such as *Rainbow Fish* by Marcus Pfister.

Though what goes on at school may form the basis of supporting the value of mutual respect and tolerance, it is vital that you, as a teacher, communicate with parents about their child's wellbeing with regard to such matters. This recognises your pastoral responsibility as a teacher linked to supporting this value. You have a responsibility to promote common shared values between parents/carers and teachers with regard to this topic. Through your pastoral work you can alert parents and carers when a child becomes the centre of such intolerance or even becomes the perpetrator of such unacceptable actions. You can suggest strategies that both the school and parents can work on to support the elimination of such unacceptable behaviours. Remember that whilst a child is in a teacher's care, the teacher takes on an *in loco parentis* role to behave and respond as any responsible parent would.

Children's widening awareness

Many opportunities can be developed that can lead to chances to explore children's widening awareness of the need for this value as this case study shows.

──────── CASE STUDY: THE UGLY DUCKLING ────────

Be alert to safeguarding issues arising with this work.

A Key Stage 1 class has just heard the traditional tale of the Ugly Duckling. It is interesting to watch their faces as the story progresses. Their sympathies are clearly (as the story intends them to be) with the ugly duckling being so different. They readily understand the pathos here. When the teacher asks them about how the ugly duckling is feeling, they are of one voice: he's 'sad', 'upset', 'feels left out'. One child offers the word 'rejected' and this leads to a short sharing of times when the children may have felt like this. Many cite small instances with brothers, sisters or friends. None of them have had to endure the experience of being rejected because of their race or skin colour – and yet they clearly can 'feel' the ugly duckling's pain. Their sympathy is almost – but not quite – empathy. Perhaps because of this, they start to say why the ugly duckling was ostracised, seeing how innocently the situation occurred. They say: 'The other ducklings didn't know how to play with him because maybe he didn't play in the same way.' One child says: 'If he had waited around and not gone off, they'd have all realised he was special' and they'd have liked him. The teacher tries gently to guide the class to think about our responsibility to others. The children don't see a problem: none of them thinks they would ever behave in the way the ducklings and other animals did.

──────── KEY QUESTIONS ────────

- How would you have used this story to illustrate the value of tolerance and to alert children to the fact that this is a British Value?
- How could the teacher have developed this opportunity to move the children's thinking beyond a fixed mind-set that they would never behave in this way to someone who was different?

This story is full of possibilities for discussing the value of tolerance, a way into helping even very young children to start to think about individual and group behaviours. In this scenario, it opened up a wealth of possibilities for teaching and learning that might have been successfully used to develop a whole series of lessons. For example, and most crucially, the young children here could not 'own' the bad behaviour of the other ducklings and relate it to themselves. All children are very conscious of giving 'right' answers and don't want to be seen in a bad light. At this stage, the focus of teaching is really on being accepting, and tolerant. This is a crucial foundation to later work which may need to cover behaviours we don't and cannot tolerate. A good follow-on strategy could have been to show a series of other pictures of different children in different scenarios and ask, 'What could you do here to make this child feel happy?' This inculcates good responses and demonstrates practical ways to show good citizenship through tolerance. The teacher could have then set the challenge of noticing and reporting all the times other children have been tolerant and kind to them or to each other in the class and in the playground. Young children love this and are willing ambassadors for this value!

Tolerance and mutual respect in school life

This value aligns well with a desire to encourage pupils to consider the need to live in a safe, accepting world, a world where they explore and accept similarities and difference in a respectful manner. The following case study exemplifies this point.

CASE STUDY: MUTUAL RESPECT AND TOLERANCE

In Year 2 the class were studying Botswana as a distant locality. The children were using a photopack to find out about the culture and life of people who lived there. They talked about the people, landscapes, weather and animals, noting similarities and differences to their own lives. As the teacher observed the children's discussion, she became concerned when she heard some negative comments (Martin, 2005). Some children were heard saying, 'the children in Africa have no clean water', 'they all live in mud huts', 'they can't afford to buy glass for their windows'. As a consequence, the teacher responded by addressing these misconceptions with the children in the following lesson. She did this by using a wide range of photographs and images representing a diverse range of landscapes, homes and places, including large cities as well as small rural communities. The children were able to see that there were many different kinds of homes, a variety of landscapes and people throughout the African continent. The focus shifted from looking at differences to looking at similarities, such as we all live in houses, we all have doors and windows in our homes. The teacher used further questioning to explore why the children thought there was no clean water. This misconception arose from TV charity advertising. The teacher reinforced that this is just one view and set it in the context of other perspectives where families had access to clean water. Gradually children were able to think about other viewpoints and understand that people live in different ways, have different beliefs and views. This was a starting point for children to learn about respecting people who are different to them. The teacher noticed that respect from the children was evident in the way they now started to talk about people in the photographs and how they linked to their own experiences.

KEY QUESTIONS

- How can you help children to develop mutual respect and tolerance through discussion? What opportunities are there to build on similarities between their lives and others who may have a different lifestyle?
- How can you use secondary sources to explore different cultures and develop understanding and respect for other people and places?

This scenario raises issues about where children get their preconceived ideas from. At times, negative images from the media can present a single story – but not the whole story – about a place, people or a culture. That is not to say that the images are wrong, but they do only present one view. A way for young children to relate to this is for them to think of their own experiences, and how they can just consider one aspect of an experience. A powerful way to learn is through linking the affective and cognitive aspects of thinking, to associate feelings and thinking (Martin, 2006). Children need support to develop an understanding of different people and places. To do this, teachers need to be responsive and prepared to challenge misconceptions that children may have, and the confidence to address potentially sensitive issues. There will be more senior and experienced staff in school who will offer support to the newer members of staff. They will have deeper knowledge of local communities, families and events.

Promoting teaching about the value of mutual respect and tolerance

Tolerance is possibly the easiest of the British Values to teach directly since its relevance and obvious links to our everyday life are easily drawn. It speaks to children's natural sense of justice and fair play. It also arises in everyday situations in the playground, classroom and outside of school, giving ample opportunities for organic conversations. As outlined previously, the value of tolerance features directly in the PHSCE curriculum and in day-to-day living and learning. Another great thing about this value is that it covers a multitude of issues and situations, all the way from politeness and good manners through to the nub issue of extremism. In fact, it is difficult not to teach about tolerance! A greater challenge for both the teacher and pupils is, arguably, about how rapidly we can move from thinking about tolerance to understanding its value. Richardson (2015) suggests that it is now a priority that teachers talk to each other. In this way a shared understanding can be agreed. However, of equal priority and of value is the need for teachers to talk to their local communities, to seek clarity at a grassroots level, as well as seeking clarity at a national level. Richardson (2015, p.44) states quite explicitly that the whole school community needs to be involved in discussions:

> *The conversation needs to involve communities, parents, pupils, and governors, and is vital at school level for taking ownership of what it means to develop a broad and balanced curriculum, and for helping to map a pathway into the future.*

To promote such understanding it is therefore important that you should make learning meaningful by giving it a personalised base, where the learner can connect on an emotional level. Give children opportunities to reflect on situations where they need to understand and tolerate themselves. Children often become painfully aware of what they perceive to be their own shortcomings; help them to be kind to themselves and to be proud of whatever natural gifts and talents they possess.

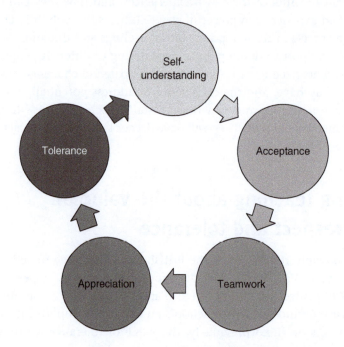

Figure 5.1 Promoting mutual respect and tolerance

If we are successfully to tackle the Prevent agenda and therefore promote this value, it may be best to consider a whole school focus on the general application of tolerance within your school. This can be achieved via the many connected values and applications that make this value worth exploring, as shown in Figure 5.1.

Values into action!

A whole school approach like this should promote strategies that allow for class discussion aimed at promoting self-awareness and understanding. This could include the following:

- using circle time to get children to think when are they most tolerant or getting them to examine their own motives for responding in the way they do to any issue around difference;

- allowing children to consider how tolerance is necessary for living together in harmony. This could be promoted, for example, by inviting pupils to look at what happens when geese fly in formation (a quick web search will yield images to support this). Talk about how we need one another and, that when we make the most of each other's attributes, we are stronger as a result.

- promoting independent thinking. Don't go along, blindly accepting the received view; stress the importance of thinking for yourself using stories such as Hans Christian Anderson's *The Emperor's New Clothes*, which makes this point wonderfully – and primary-aged children adore its risqué nature!

- allowing pupils to develop empathy: share with pupils a situation when you have been a stranger, perhaps at a party or a meeting. Use scenarios to develop this quality; for example, ask the children how they would have felt in the situation. Now ask the children to imagine that they are among the guests already in the room. When they notice the newcomer, what will they do? Ask the new person to join their group? Ignore the new person and continue talking with their own friends? Hope the stranger will go away? Expect someone else to talk to the newcomer? Help the children to identify some of the problems of being new. The other people may have different rules about behaviour, different ways of doing things, different jokes. Help the pupils to see that being 'on the outside' is not easy and we need to show our understanding. Children, of course, can be very good at accepting differences – let us not overlook that in our attempts to 'teach' them! You could also consider using resources such as 'A Mile in His Moccasins', a poem attributed to various American Indian tribes (and quickly found through a web search), to explore further the need for tolerance and understanding;

- getting children to consider whether there is a time when we should not be tolerant. This is where discussion about safeguarding issues, extremist views and religious intolerance may come into play. As teachers and educators we need to be aware that tolerance has its limits and, in order to be safe in the world, our pupils also need to be aware of this. Fairy stories can provide a gentle lead-in to this; for example, discussion about Cinderella's treatment at the hands of her step-mother would not be tolerated today – or would it and is it? In Hansel and Gretel, should the father have been much less tolerant of his wife and her behaviour to the children? When do we need to stand up for ourselves and for others?

A SUMMARY OF KEY POINTS FROM THIS CHAPTER

- With the ethnically diverse society in which we live there is a need to be tolerant and to show mutual respect to one another.
- Intolerance should be challenged and dealt with effectively to promote an inclusive, harmonious society.
- By engaging in the essence of this value, children can develop empathy with others so they can form part of an inclusive school and community.
- There is a statutory responsibility for schools to promote mutual respect and tolerance of others' differences.
- Teachers are required, as part of the Teachers' Standards, to help to promote mutual respect and tolerance.
- Relationships provide the key to promoting this value successfully.
- Schools can make direct links to the National Curriculum and its requirements with this value. It can also be integrated into the wider organisation and management of the school.
- Teachers need to be alert to where the concept can arise unexpectedly and maximise these opportunities whilst being mindful of safeguarding issues.
- Schools must be mindful of safeguarding issues in relation to teaching about this area of British Values, and must be cognisant of their duties to report any suspected radicalisation.

References

Bhopal, K. and Myers, M. (2009) 'Gypsy, Roma and Traveller pupils in schools in the UK: inclusion and good practice'. *International Journal of Inclusive Education*, 13 (3): 299–314.

Bhopal, K. and Rhamie, J. (2014) 'Initial teacher training: understanding race, diversity and inclusion'. *Race, Ethnicity and Education*, 17 (3): 304–25.

Biale, E. Galeotti, E. and Liveriero, F. (2017) 'Introduction: democracy, diversity'. *Critical Review of International Social and Political Philosophy*, 20 (4): 1–8.

Carroll, J. and Alexander, G.N. (2016) *The Teachers' Standards in Primary School. Understanding and Evidencing Effective Practice*. London: SAGE.

Department for Education (2012) Teachers' Standards. DFE-00066-2011. London: Department for Education.

Department for Education (2014a) Promoting fundamental British Values as part of SMSC in Schools. Available at: https://www.gov.uk/government/uploads/system/uploads/attachment_data/file/380595/SMSC_Guidance_Maintained_Schools.pdf (accessed 10 July 2017).

Department for Education (2014b) The Equality Act 2010 and schools. Departmental advice for school leaders, school staff, governing bodies and local authorities. Available at: https://www.gov.uk/government/uploads/system/uploads/attachment_data/file/315587/Equality_Act_Advice_Final.pdf (accessed 10 July 2017).

Department for Education (2016) EU Referendum Result Department for Education Update. Available at: https://www.gov.uk/government/news/eu-referendum-result-department-for-education-update (accessed 12 December 2017).

Elton-Chalcraft, S., Linder, V., Revell, L., Warner, D. and Whitworth, L. (2017) 'To promote, or not to promote fundamental British Values? Teachers' Standards, diversity and teacher education'. *British Educational Research Journal*, 43 (1): 29–48.

Martin, F. (2005) 'Photographs don't speak'. *Primary Geographer*, Spring: pp.7–11.

Martin, F. (2006) 'Everyday geography'. *Primary Geographer*, Autumn : pp.4–7.

Maylor, U. (2016) '"I'd worry about how to teach it": British Values in English classrooms'. *Journal of Education for Teaching*, 42 (3): 314–28.

Pigozzi, M.J. (2006) 'A UNESCO view of global citizenship education'. *Educational Review*, 58 (1): 1–4.

Richardson, R. (2015) 'British Values and British identity'. *London Review of Education*, 13 (2): 37–48.

UNESCO (1989) Convention on the Rights of the Child. Available at: http://www.unesco.org/education/pdf/CHILD_E.PDF (accessed 11 June 2017).

Woolley, R. (2013) 'Values'. In: Taylor, K. and Woolley, R. (eds), *Values and Vision in Primary Education*. Maidenhead: McGraw Hill Education/Open University Press, pp.189–206.

Further reading

Hicks, P.P. and Thomas, G. (2008) *Inclusion and Diversity in Education*. London: SAGE.

Woolley, R. (ed.) (2018) *Understanding Inclusion: Core Concepts, Policy and Practice*. Abingdon: Routledge.

Useful websites to use to support teaching about mutual respect and tolerance

Centre for Studies on Inclusive Education. Available at: http://www.csie.org.uk/inclusion/what.shtml (accessed 13 July 2017).

Global Dimension. Available at: https://globaldimension.org.uk/resource/dollar-street

National Association of Language Development in the Curriculum (NALDIC). Available at https://www.naldic.org.uk/eal-initial-teacher-education/ite-programmes/eal-sen/ (accessed 13 July 2017).

Respect Assembly. Available at: http://www.assemblies.org.uk/sec/1484/respect (accessed 10 July 2017).

6

A WHOLE SCHOOL APPROACH TO BRITISH VALUES

This chapter explores:

- the rationale behind a whole school approach to British Values;
- why and how the leadership and management of a school should promote such an approach;
- the importance of the school's ethos, culture, curriculum, practice and learning environment in promoting a unified approach to British Values;
- the role of children and young people in this approach;
- how continuing professional development underpins the successful whole school approach;
- how a partnership between parents, carers and outside agencies is vital in supporting British Values.

Teachers' Standards

This chapter supports the development of the following Teachers' Standards:

TS8: Fulfil wider professional responsibilities:

- take responsibility for improving teaching through appropriate professional development, responding to advice and feedback from colleagues.

Part Two: Personal and professional conduct

Teachers uphold public trust in the profession and maintain high standards of ethics and behaviour, within and outside school, by:

- treating pupils with dignity, building relationships rooted in mutual respect, and at all times observing proper boundaries appropriate to a teacher's professional position;

- having regard for the need to safeguard pupils' wellbeing, in accordance with statutory provisions;

- showing tolerance of and respect for the rights of others;

- not undermining fundamental British Values, including democracy, the rule of law, individual liberty and mutual respect, and tolerance of those with different faiths and beliefs;

- ensuring that personal beliefs are not expressed in ways which exploit pupils' vulnerability or might lead them to break the law;

- teachers must have an understanding of, and always act within, the statutory frameworks which set out their professional duties and responsibilities.

Introduction

This chapter will focus on the need for a whole school approach to British Values. It will examine the role that leadership and management can play in setting and promoting a clear, agreed policy to underpin such an approach. It will examine how the creation of such a policy may serve to inform and shape school practice. This may be seen in terms of the setting's ethos, culture, learning environment, curriculum and professional practice. Additionally, there is a recognition of the important place that children and young people and their voice can have in promoting this value. Finally, the role of teachers' continuing professional development will be considered as a means of enhancing practice. Alongside this, the partnership between parents, carers and outside agencies will be outlined for the vital role it plays in supporting the successful delivery of this set of values.

Why a whole school approach to British Values?

Schools initially had many concerns linked to the idea of promoting the concept of 'British Values'.

KEY QUESTION

- Why were some schools initially concerned with the idea of promoting British Values?

These concerns were generally centred on the notion that the place of these values in education and society was something rather unique, or as being a representation of what stereotypical Britishness should be. Further to this, at the very macro-scale of society, British Values' place in schools was driven by a statutory ambition to prevent terrorism as part of the Prevent agenda rather than that of a more general approach to education. Also such British Values were underpinned by governmental concerns regarding their loss as a result of the ethnic community's commitment to their own values in our society (Maylor, 2016). As Maylor (2016, p.319) indicates, British Values were the government's attempt to:

engender and some might argue indoctrinate (minority ethnic) commitment to British values, so as to maintain control of minority ethnic communities by ensuring that teachers demand commitments to British values through the curriculum and their teaching approach to minority ethnic communities.

Given such an agenda, British Values were therefore sometimes viewed as perhaps leading to the creation of divisions, alienation and suspicion among individuals in society. With such concerns, it is understandable that for some schools this stance seemingly ran contrary to a whole school's wish to be inclusive, nurturing and welcoming. Within this context is the view that schools should be a place where individual difference should be celebrated and encouraged.

Universal values

Despite such initial misgivings, British Values of democracy, individual liberty, rule of law and mutual respect and tolerance have been successfully integrated into the whole school daily approach with great speed and success. This successful embedding and support for promoting these fundamental British Values in our schools can be linked to the idea that they are often seen as 'universal values' and values that have a direct link to the Universal Declaration of Human Rights (NASWUT and EqualiTeach CIC, 2017). As such, and given their part of this national initiative, schools have worked hard to promote these values in terms of the role that they give our children and young people to 'explore, understand and celebrate their own personal and social identity and the identities of others' (NASWUT and EqualiTeach CIC, 2017, p.7).

It could be argued, however, that the inception of what underpins the ideals of 'British Values' has always happened in schools and such an agenda of promoting issues such as mutual respect and tolerance has been taken seriously by schools. This has happened because of a school's need to educate children and young people to live in what may be seen as our diverse nation, where cultures, faiths, religions and beliefs vary significantly, as do social backgrounds. The uniqueness of schools has meant that each setting faces its own particular challenges in instilling such values due to individual demographics and ever-changing pupil composition. However, for schools to be successful, whatever their differences, they have always given children and young people the opportunity to appreciate diversity. This is through the interaction with others who may have differences as well as sharing similarities. To consider difference, to challenge inequality and ignorance and to share values is an enabling experience, allowing for discussion about their different and common experiences and opinions. Therefore, the successful promotion of a whole school approach to these values was surely in place before the inception of such a statutory requirement was conceived. What may now be argued to have happened in schools is that these values have been aligned to the government requirement to promote British Values. Schools' current good practice relating to core values such as mutual respect and tolerance encompasses the requirement of the statutory approach to British Values. This has also meant that schools have been successful in supporting their other statutory duties embedded in such a policy – for example, the need to promote community cohesion (Department of Children and Family Services, 2007); Section 149 of the Equality Act 2010 to promote equal and the removal of discrimination; and the Prevent duty (Department for Education, 2015) to prevent radicalisation.

The benefits for pupils

KEY QUESTION

- How can the promotion of British Values in school impact children's lives in a positive way?

By promoting British Values schools can provide children and young people with a positive identity and learning opportunities, as well as the skills needed to mediate against life's challenges linked to the corruption of such values. It can help individuals to become more resilient to and navigate away from the range of factors that can damage their wish to adhere to such values. These can include, for example, peer pressure and the sometimes damaging effects of media reporting. By the promotion of a whole school approach to British Values it can serve to support children and young people with school-based strategies, which therefore allows for a holistic drive to support the pressure against the deterioration of such values. The principles of those beliefs included in British Values would seem to be shared by OFSTED which has placed such considerations in its Common Inspection Framework (OFSTED, 2015b) when judging the quality of leadership and management. By OFSTED's monitoring of the provision in schools, by their examining of a range of records – for example, bullying, racism and homophobia incidents (OFSTED, 2015a, p.51) – OFSTED wishes not only to ensure that British Values are being adhered to, but also children's and young people's physical, emotional health, safety and wellbeing are also being looked after.

What does a whole school approach to British Values look like?

Most importantly, it needs outstanding leadership and management which can create a shared ethos within the school in order to support the promotion of such ideals, as well as encouraging effective practice. Such macro-commitment is vital if such an approach is able to filter down to the best of class-based practice as well as creating a culture of responsibility and belonging for individuals. All elements of this approach and practice should be nourished by an effective curriculum and pupils who feel empowered to challenge injustices and to champion British Values. It should have parents and a wider school community who can buy into these values and support such a whole school focus on their promotion. Finally, for some, staff training will also provide a means of enhancing the delivery of these values by allowing teachers to reflect upon and challenge the misconceptions linked to such issues as the law, individual liberty, mutual respect and tolerance of different faiths and beliefs.

Figure 6.1 illustrates the central role that a whole school approach to British Values should play in school life as well as the contributory factors needed to maximise its effectiveness.

Such a model's conception is linked to that of Bronfenbrenner (1979) and Bronfenbrenner's Model (after Knoff, 1984, in Frederickson and Cline, 2003), which sees an individual's development as being at the heart of the relationship to their immediate school environment. In this model elements such as leadership and management and the school culture feed into the central development of a child's education and safety, underpinned by British Values and Prevent. The 'macro-system' or outer layer of this model reflects the 'possible blueprints for the future as reflected in the vision of a society's political leaders' (Bronfenbrenner, 1979, p.26) which, in this case, relates to the Prevent agenda and the promotion of British Values. These macro-expectations are embedded and promoted through government

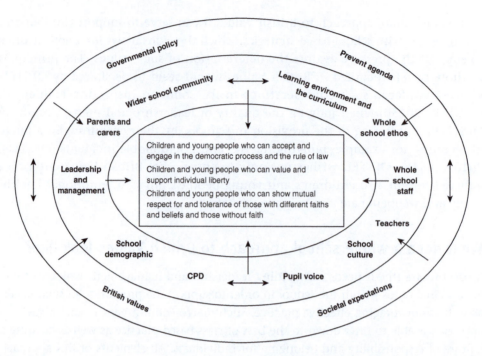

Figure 6.1 The central role that a whole school approach to British Values plays in child's school life

documentation such as the Teachers' Standards. As Maylor (2016, p.318) indicates, such standards serve to frame government expectations so as to suggest:

> *that British values are viewed by the government as much more than ideologies that guide human behaviour. Instead, they are considered central to maintaining community cohesion and preventing the seeds of radicalism and terrorism being sown in the minds of pupils.*

However, it is important to realise that such macro-expectations for these values will be subject to change over time and that what is purported to be effective in today's anti-radicalisation agenda will inevitably alter with societal events.

Leadership and management

Leadership and management must be surely seen as vital in holding a strategic position in a school's development, as well as being pivotal in planning for and bringing about whole school change. Such a whole school policy provides the basis for a climate and ethos which challenges and encourages the successful promotion of British Values. It will forge a school approach where diversity is celebrated and accepted.

It will also allow children to feel secure, know they are valued as individuals and provide a safe environment away from emotional and physical harm where honest and open discussion can happen – a place where relationships between the teacher and the pupils will be positive so as to give children a voice to speak out and challenge injustices. It is important to remember that the expectations for the delivery of this agenda by leadership and management will be monitored by OFSTED in their inspection documentation (OFSTED, 2015a, 2015b), so evidencing your strategy and success is vital.

It is important that such clear policy expectations by school leaders regarding the promotion and delivery of these values in schools, as viewed on schools' websites, do not sit in isolation from other school policies. Other aspects of a school's work that may also support children and young people in this aspect of their lives may be found in embedded in policies such as:

- inclusion;
- PSHE;
- anti-bullying;
- e-safety;
- safeguarding;
- values;
- equality and diversity.

However, it is vital that before any such whole school approach can become effective in any setting, as with other initiatives, leaders promote a shared understanding and commitment for such a focus. Maylor (2016) noted that not all teachers had a shared understanding of British Values and that, importantly, the significance of these values for a school changed as a result of the settings demographics. This makes a review of a whole school approach vital so that it best supports the context in which you have to teach about such issues. Any discussion, however, should not be about how closely pupils align to perceived 'Britishness' with regard to British Values, but it should be about 'honest debates about British values and whether they are shared or not' (Maylor, 2016, p.323).

Questions that might be needed to facilitate such elements of effective whole school British Values might include the following:

- What is your consistently understood definition of these core British Values?
- What are our key priorities and actions needed to promote these values as a whole school approach?

- Are there any key values that are more challenging than others to promote in your setting?

- Who in the school should be accountable for British Values and what are your priorities?

- How are children and young people, parents/carers and external partners given a voice in the promotion of British Values in our setting?

The leadership and management of the school may wish to use processes such as the Values-based Education Quality Mark (www.valuesbasededucation.com) or the Rights Respecting Schools Award (https://www.unicef.org.uk/rights-respecting-schools/) to underpin their work and to put children's rights at the heart of whole school development. Such work would not only make children aware of the vital importance of the United Nations Convention on the Rights of the Child, but also how such work can underpin whole school values and policies. It can serve to promote a rights-respecting and values-based ethos, as well as helping children's empowerment to be active learners and citizens.

Curriculum planning and practice

KEY QUESTION

- How can the promotion of British Values be integrated into the curriculum?

Many opportunities can be provided by schools to promote and develop social and emotional skills to support British Values, not only through their use of personal social, health and economic education (PSHE) and their social, moral, spiritual and cultural (SMSC) provision, but also through the wider curriculum. It is important that such work is valued and has significance. Therefore British Values should not form a separate entity in the life of the school but should be integral to a holistic whole school approach to such values and the delivery of SMSC in your school. By re-evaluating your current practice and schemes of work, it may easily be possible to integrate British Values into the day-to-day life of the school with minor modifications to current practice.

As discussed in the preceding chapters, each British Value may be underpinned by work in curricular areas such as English, history and religious education. Assemblies may form the basis of exploring British Values, as well as enhancement activities such as school trips or multicultural or faith days. Anti-bullying and diversity activities, alongside the work of the

School Council, may strengthen a school's work on British Values. Similarly, high-quality displays may seek to raise awareness of the importance of these values.

SMSC is perceived by OFSTED (2015a) as an important aspect of an individual's development and should be seen alongside PSHE as a vital strategy in promoting British Values. SMSC may be found in school in many aspects of the taught curriculum such as cultural development through religious education, as well as through opportunities such as circle time, where issues such as difference can be discussed. As the Department for Education (2014) suggests with regard to SMSC, it can seek to promote concepts such as respect for others and the democratic process, in addition to tolerance for other cultures and the rule of law.

As children grow into young people, SMSC British Values may be promoted in terms of a 'citizenship curriculum'. This forms part of the Key Stage 3 and 4 curriculum which serves to ensure that an individual can make a valuable contribution to our world. It also facilitates children and young people gaining the skills, knowledge and understanding to form valued members of society.

Schools can use resources such as the PSHE Association programmes of study (PSHE Association, 2015) on health and wellbeing, relationships and living in the wider world (PHSE Association, 2015, p.5) to help underpin their work on British Values which can also help a school's development and understanding of issues such as diversity, relationship and equality.

LIFE IN MODERN BRITAIN

At our primary school we take very seriously our responsibility to prepare children for life in modern Britain. We ensure that fundamental British Values are introduced, discussed and lived out through our commitment to a values-based philosophy that infuses the ethos and work of the school. All curriculum areas provide a vehicle for furthering understanding of these concepts and, in particular, our religious education, SMSC, PSHE, citizenship and philosophy lessons provide excellent opportunities to deepen and develop understanding. Children embrace these concepts with enthusiasm and demonstrate a good understanding of their application to their own lives.

The school makes considerable efforts to ensure children have exposure to a wide experience beyond their local community during which these concepts are shown, through, for example, sporting events, residential visits to other localities and outdoor centres and through visiting speakers from other denominations and groups. Their strong-rooted values-based understanding gives them an excellent platform for embracing difference.

Values into action!

School leaders often find that carrying out an audit of provision is an efficient and effective way to ensure that practice is as good as it can be. There is no reason why a teacher should not also do this, using a simple template such as that in Table 6.1.

The voice of children and young people

Given the nature of British Values it is vital that the child's voice is heard when considering issues such as tolerance and mutual respect. It is important to note that freedom of expression is also a right under Article 12 of the United Nations Convention on the Rights of the Child: 'Children have the right to express their views freely and for their views to be given due weight in matters affecting them' (Robinson, 2014, p.18).

As a teacher wishing to promote inclusion and diversity, you should realise that it is often those who are most marginalised who may sometimes find it hard to be heard and therefore may need listening to the most. If children and young people are to feel a connection to and ownership of British Values they must be involved in meaningful dialogue, as well as contributing to this school agenda. Curriculum-based strategies such as PSHE and circle time may provide a means to explore pupils' views on values-related issues and to give them the opportunity to challenge and understand such concepts. Groups such as school councils should not only represent the range of individuals in a setting but they should be taught and be given the skills necessary to challenge inequality and promote democracy. Authors such as Robinson (2014) note that, in schools that take a rights-respecting approach, there may a reduction in incidents of bullying, as well as an enhanced ability for individuals to deal with conflicts they come across. Children and young people who encounter a rights-respecting approach feel valued, respected, cared for and listened to (Robinson, 2014). Good practice should be embedded in relationships with staff where genuine concern is shown towards individuals' wellbeing.

Other school-based strategies that a setting might provide to promote a pupil's voice include the following:

- presenting topical issues at assemblies;

- opportunities to promote equality and diversity through eco-council work or concepts such as Fair Trade stalls or Wateraid;

- working towards quality marks such as the Rights Respecting Schools Award or the Values-based Education Quality Mark.

Table 6.1 A whole school audit

British Value	Statement	Evidence	Impact
Mutual tolerance of those with different faiths and beliefs	Respect is a fundamental school value, around which pivots much of the work of the school. A baseline for a fair community is that each person's right to 'be themselves' is accepted by all. However, tolerance may on its own not be enough: our values-based framework and approach to religious education can challenge pupils to be increasingly respectful and to celebrate diversity. We pay explicit attention to this as part of our religious education, PHSE and SMSC curriculum. Respect is a school value that is discussed deeply, starting with self-respect and covering: respect for family, friends and other groups; the world and its people; and the environment.	• Records of P4C sessions • Collective Worship planning and outcomes file • Religious Education curriculum • Religious Education planning and work books • 'Learning walks' for behaviour and behaviour for learning • School Values programme • Curriculum planning • PSHE programme, including safeguarding • British Values teaching resources used and writing/work resulting from this	Children can articulate why tolerance is important; how they show respect to others and how they feel about it themselves. Children's behaviour demonstrates their good understanding of this value in action. Children are able to talk about the different faiths and cultures they learn about, ask questions and show tolerance and respect for others of different faiths and religions.
Respectful attitudes	Our values-based approach to learning focuses on developing mutual respect between those of different faiths and beliefs, promoting an understanding that society gains from diversity. Pupils learn about diversity in religions and worldviews and will be challenged to respect other persons who see the world differently to themselves. Recognition and celebration of human diversity in many forms can flourish where pupils understand different faiths and beliefs, and are challenged to be broad-minded and open-hearted.	• Records of P4C sessions • Collective Worship planning and outcomes file • Religious Education curriculum • Religious Education planning and work books • 'Learning walks' for behaviour and behaviour for learning • School Values programme • PSHE programme, including safeguarding • Curriculum planning • British Values teaching resources used and writing/work resulting from this.	Children can readily articulate why respect is important, how they show respect to others and how they feel about it themselves. Children's behaviour demonstrates their good understanding of this value in action. Children are able to talk about the different faiths and cultures they learn about, ask questions and show tolerance and respect for others of different faiths and religions.

(Continued)

Table 6.1 (Continued)

British Value	Statement	Evidence	Impact
Democracy	The children at this school see democracy borne out in a whole variety of ways and see this as being an essential component of successful team working. Democracy is a school value that children meet when discussing respect and fairness. In religious education and P4C pupils learn the significance of each person's ideas and experiences through discussion. In debating the fundamental questions of life, pupils learn to respect a range of perspectives. This contributes to learning about democracy, examining the idea that we all share responsibility to use our voice and influence for the wellbeing of others.	• School Council minutes and records • Records of P4C sessions • Collective Worship planning and outcomes file • Religious Education planning and work books • 'Learning walks' for behaviour and behaviour for learning • School Values programme • PSHE programme, including safeguarding • Curriculum planning • British Values teaching resources used and writing/work resulting from this	Children are able to work cooperatively in pairs and groups, as well as in whole class situations. They understand about turn-taking and respecting the views of others. Children in KS2, in particular, are able to use the language of respect – e.g. 'I agree with/I don't agree with ...' through their philosophy training. Fundraising for charities at home and abroad to feel connection with those from different cultures.
Rule of law	The children at this school are familiar with this concept through the strong values-based philosophy that infuses the entire work of the school. They are familiar with the concept too through the discussion of our Christian values and, in religious education lessons, the idea that different religions have guiding principles. Children are used to debating and discussing laws/rules and their application. Children are familiar with the local police, who take assemblies and talk to them informally.	• Class rules • School code of conduct/learning behaviours • School Values • PSHE/Citizenship lessons on the role of law and Parliament (see visit from Bill Wiggins, MP) • School Council minutes and records • Records of P4C sessions • Collective Worship planning and outcomes file	Children are able to articulate how and why we need to behave in school and demonstrate they understand and can abide by these. KS2 children understand why we have laws, how these work and how the rule of law relates to their own lives. They are able to discuss and debate philosophical issues in relation to these.

British Value	Statement	Evidence	Impact
	In religious education pupils examine different examples of codes for human life, including commandments and rules or precepts offered by different religious communities. They learn to appreciate how to apply these ideas to their own communities. They learn that fairness requires the law to apply equally to all	• Religious Education planning and work books • 'Learning walks' for behaviour and behaviour for learning • School Values programme • PSHE programme, including safeguarding • Curriculum planning • British Values teaching resources used and writing/work resulting from this	
Individual liberty	Our values-based discussions and acts of worship begin with discussion about the self – e.g. self-respect and self-worth in relation to individual value; children see that they are important in their own right. The philosophy of our teaching and learning places emphasis on the right to have our own thoughts and evidence-based views. Children are strongly encouraged to develop independence in learning and to think for themselves. In religious education pupils consider questions about identity, belonging and diversity, learning what it means to live a life free from constraints. They study examples of pioneers of human freedoms, including those from within different religions, so that they can examine tensions between the value of a stable society and the value of change for human development.	• Class rules • School code of conduct/learning behaviours • School Values • PSHE/Citizenship lessons on the role of law and Parliament (see visit from Bill Wiggins, MP) • School Council minutes and records • Records of P4C sessions • Collective Worship planning and outcomes file • Religious Education planning and work books • 'Learning walks' for behaviour and behaviour for learning • School Values programme • PSHE programme, including safeguarding • Curriculum planning • British Values teaching resources used and writing/work resulting from this	Children understand about the importance of accepting responsibility and of their right to be heard in school. They are consulted on many aspects of school life and demonstrate independence of thought and action.

Partnership with parents, carers and outside agencies

---- **KEY QUESTION** ----

- How can schools develop successful partnerships with parents and carers to promote British Values?

Given the diverse demographic, socio-economic and cultural background from which schools draw their pupils, each school will have its own clear strategic priorities to promote successful partnership with parents, foster carers and members of extended families in order to promote British Values. Such work will be based on the need to support what is a huge range of understanding of the term 'British identity'. For any looked-after children, such links can play a vital pivotal role in supporting them in the face of issues in the home setting, with the school setting offering security. Good practice, as indicated by OFSTED (2015a), therefore suggests that schools engage with parents and carers in order to support their child/young person's safety and SMSC development alongside guidance to help support their improvement. The key to such success will need to be based on open, honest and welcoming relationships, where opportunities linked to expertise from people such as parents or their extended family are used to strengthen bonds and promote an understanding of tolerance for other cultures, faiths and beliefs. School must also play a pivotal role in the community which they serve and support local initiatives to promote diversity and inclusion.

Allied to this is a need for schools to seek help when needed from external partnerships such as social workers, so as to allow leaders to identify and support children and young people effectively (OFSTED, 2015a). Outside speakers from the community can be used to promote an understanding of topics such as the rule of law by involving the police or the local MP, alongside visits to religious sites such as mosques to explore the notion of diversity and differences in faith.

It is also vital that parents, foster parents, carers and members of extended families also buy into the promotion of British Values in their schools. Therefore schools will need to be open, honest and transparent with them about the agenda they are promoting when undertaking this work. As well as providing opportunities to come into school to see how these values are being tackled and to receive focused input, such as through parents' evenings about the role and importance of British Values in any particular setting, such work may also provide valuable opportunities to challenge parental misconceptions or negative stereotyping.

Continuing professional development (CPD)

Teachers, especially the Designated Safeguarding lead, will have had Prevent training to support their awareness and protection of children at risk of radicalisation (Department for Education, 2015). However, studies such as Maylor (2016, p.324) clearly note issues around the conceptualisation of identity linked to Britishness for teachers, as well as some teaching professionals exhibiting a lack of tolerance and understanding of minority ethnic groups due to their ill-informed views about these groups of individuals.

Given these points, for any CPD to be effective it must be founded on a clear assessment of a teacher's professional needs as well as on what is needed to support whole school improvement. This could be achieved through the use of a school's performance management systems. Ultimately, this provides a formal setting in which to encourage, challenge and support teachers' improvement (OFSTED, 2015a).

Although the training teachers often receive will not directly be labelled as that of British Values and the Prevent agenda, it is important that curriculum and staff upskilling and awareness training takes place in order to inform effective practice in schools.

This could include the following:

- training linked to the safeguarding of individuals around issues of radicalisation provided by the Child Exploitation and Online Protection Command (CEOP);

- whole school curriculum development to develop a better understanding for a range of faiths;

- child protection/safeguarding training linked to issues around vulnerable groups such as migrants;

- individual's own CPD awareness-raising can also be promoted by visiting websites such as Liberty and Amnesty International.

Conclusion

A clear message has been conveyed, by government, that schools must not undermine British Values (Department for Education, 2014). This has been interpreted by headteachers, governors and teachers and implemented in daily practice to ensure children are kept safe, potential issues concerning radicalisation are addressed and misconceptions about other cultures and beliefs are challenged. The four British Values, identified by the government, of rule of law, democracy, liberty, and mutual respect and tolerance have been defined and discussed. Whilst the term 'rule of law' is difficult to define, it has been suggested that this offers some flexibility in the way that schools evidence it through their practice. What can be agreed is that this value meets a specific purpose and, whereas it concerns the whole school community, it is also about assuming individual responsibility as an accountable member of that group. Living in a democratic society may result in a certain attitude of taking freedom for granted. As we come to question what democracy looks like in schools, it has been proposed that this value plays a significant part in daily school life. It is evident in each class, with the agreement of class rules and on a wider scale through the organisation of a school council. These examples illustrate the importance placed upon the pupil voice. Moving on to the value of liberty, it was proposed that liberty involves an individual choice being made within the rules and regulations set by the community to which they belong. The governance of that community is for the greater good, rather than about individual gain. Within schools, value is placed upon supporting children to be independent learners, to make the right choices and so make a positive contribution to their local community and to wider society. Mutual respect and tolerance may be the least complex of the British Values to understand. Perhaps this is partly due to the fact that the terms are more widely used. Two key themes are identified: one which includes maintenance of an ethos where respect between adults and children is evident through a cohesive community; the other is that of prevention of disrespect and intolerance, with a focus upon addressing and dealing assertively with potential challenges. British Values do not sit in isolation but can be found within the school ethos, the curriculum and woven throughout the daily interactions of the school community. The values are integral to promoting diversity and an inclusive environment in which all pupils feel valued. This, we suggest, is not new but has been evident over time in the good practice that has existed in effective schools. The focus now needs to centre upon providing high-quality CPD as teachers seek opportunities to discuss and share good practice. The British Values agenda continues to evolve as values are defined, examples from classrooms are shared and common agreement is reached about the shared values. The heart of the ongoing discussions draws us back to the consideration of inclusion, diversity and dealing with differences. Yet, the importance of identifying similarities must feature strongly so that children and young people can recognise and empathise with others, in order then to accept and respect difference.

The government has defined what being British means. It has been discussed that this includes having regard for British political structures, respecting the laws and upholding traditional values, including respect and tolerance. Yet, it has also been highlighted that these values may not be unique to Britain and some people view values as something personal to each individual. For the staff and pupils within schools, as well as the governors, parents and the wider school social context, being

British involves being part of a community. This is defined as a unified group who have shared values and communicate effectively with each other and who do not see difference as an issue. The effectiveness of such a community is based upon having a strong sense of commitment to the group who are cohesive; this comes from having a shared vision. Within this context the differences are accepted because they are set within a shared understanding of future goals. As a teacher, your own values will define your identity and be a driver for the kind of teacher you will develop into. Yet, alongside this, it has been highlighted that teachers must uphold public trust in the profession and through meeting the Teachers' Standards (Department for Education, 2012) they will be concerned with the wider connections to British Values.

A SUMMARY OF KEY POINTS FROM THIS CHAPTER

- In undertaking good and worthwhile teaching of British Values, you have, as a teacher, both a professional and an ethical duty.
- British Values belong to and are relevant to the whole school community at a macro-level through the Prevent agenda.
- The teaching of British Values in school is best accomplished through a whole school approach.
- Effective teaching and learning of British Values happens when it permeates the whole curriculum and is not treated as a 'bolt on' to the rest of the curriculum.
- There are a variety of tools to help you as a teacher, and schools as organisations, to really embrace this agenda and make it your own.
- Teaching British Values in the primary school can be a creative process, offering myriad ways into other subject areas and relating to pupils' self-identity, relationships and personal development.

References

Bronfenbrenner, U. (1979) *The Ecology of Human Development*. Cambridge, MA: Harvard University Press.

Department of Children and Family Services (2007) Guidance on the duty to promote community cohesion. Available at: http://webarchive.nationalarchives.gov.uk/20130321054751/https://www.education.gov.uk/publications/eOrderingDownload/DCSF-00598-2007.pdf (accessed 13 July 2017).

Department for Education (2012) Teachers' Standards. DFE-00066-2011. London: Department for Education.

Department for Education (2014) Promoting fundamental British Values as part of SMSC in schools. Available at: https://www.gov.uk/government/uploads/system/uploads/attachment_data/file/380595/SMSC_Guidance_Maintained_Schools.pdf (accessed 20 July 2017).

Department for Education (2015) The Prevent duty. Departmental advice for schools and childcare providers. Available at: https://www.gov.uk/government/uploads/system/uploads/attachment_data/file/439598/prevent-duty-departmental-advice-v6.pdf (accessed 21 July 2017).

Frederickson, N. and Cline, T. (2003) *Special Educational Needs: Inclusion and Diversity – A Textbook*. Buckingham: Open University Press.

HM Government (2015) Prevent Duty Guidance: for England and Wales. Available at: https://www.gov.uk/government/publications/prevent-duty-guidance (accessed 16 July 2017).

NASWUT and EqualiTeach CIC (2017) Responding holistically to the requirement to promote Fundamental British Values. Available at: https://www.nasuwt.org.uk/uploads/assets/uploaded/b49175fd-4bf6-4f2d-ac5b2759c03015be.pdf (accessed 15 July 2017).

OFSTED (2015a) School inspection handbook: handbook for inspecting schools in England under section 5 of the Education Act 2005. Available at: https://www.gov.uk/government/publications/school-inspection-handbook-from-september-2015 (accessed 23 December 2016).

OFSTED (2015b) The common inspection framework: education, skills and early years. Available at: https://www.gov.uk/government/uploads/system/uploads/attachment_data/file/461767/The_common_inspection_framework_education_skills_and_early_years.pdf (accessed 12 June 2017).

Maylor, U. (2016) '"I'd worry about how to teach it": British Values in English classrooms'. *Journal of Education for Teaching*, 42 (3): 314–28.

PSHE Association (2015) Teacher Guidance: Preparing to teach about mental health and emotional wellbeing. Available at: https://www.pshe-association.org.uk/curriculum-and-resources/resources/guidance-preparing-teach-about-mental-health-and (accessed 10 November 2016).

Robinson, C. (2014) 'Children, their voices and their experiences of school: What does that tell us?', Research Reports Cambridge Primary Review Trust Survey 2.

INDEX

Added to a page number 'f' denotes a figure and 't' denotes a table.